The Book of the
FORD CORTINA Mk3

Do-it-yourself Servicing and Maintenance in the Home Garage Covering the Cortina 1300, 1600, 1600GT, 2000 and 2000GT UK models

Staton Abbey, M.I.M.I.

Pitman Publishing

First published 1972

SIR ISAAC PITMAN AND SONS LTD
Pitman House, Parker Street, Kingsway, London, WC2B 5PB
P.O. Box 46038, Portal Street, Nairobi, Kenya

SIR ISAAC PITMAN (AUST.) PTY. LTD
Pitman House, 158 Bouverie Street, Carlton, Victoria 3053, Australia

PITMAN PUBLISHING COMPANY S.A. LTD
P.O. Box 11231, Johannesburg, S. Africa

PITMAN PUBLISHING CORPORATION
6 East 43rd Street, New York 10017, U.S.A.

SIR ISAAC PITMAN (CANADA) LTD
495 Wellington Street West, Toronto 135, Canada

THE COPP CLARK PUBLISHING COMPANY
517 Wellington Street West, Toronto 135, Canada

ISBN: 0 273 36181 3

Set in 8/9 pt. Monotype Times New Roman, printed
by photolithography and bound in Great Britain at
The Pitman Press, Bath
G2—(G.4197:19)

The Book of the
FORD CORTINA Mk3

A Cortina 1300, in standard form, is the first in a wide range of models which differ in engine size, power-output and trim

The L and XL version of the Cortina Mk 3. External recognition points are the bright window mouldings and the rubber inserts in the bumpers

How this book was planned

MORE and more owners are turning to do-it-yourself maintenance nowadays, and the object of this book is to make the initiation of the novice as painless as possible.

The more experienced owner, however, has not been forgotten, and the practical man will find jobs such as decarbonizing and valve grinding, ignition timing, carburettor servicing and brake relining fully described. A word of warning is given when the design of the Cortina calls for specialized knowledge or the use of service tools and equipment.

When planning new books in this series it was decided to make as much use as possible of "programmed instruction," which allows a complex technical job to be broken down into a series of easy, logical steps, so that even a novice can tackle the work with confidence. Maintenance or servicing jobs have therefore been analysed under three headings:

Information: the reasons for doing the work, and an outline of the basic theory in non-technical terms; this will often be helpful in maintenance, fault-tracing or adjustment.

Operation: the bare bones of the job, briefly described in simple step-by-step form, without confusing details.

Explanation: supplementary notes on how to do the work, including practical tips for the beginner, pitfalls to avoid and whether any special tools will be needed.

Grateful thanks are due to the Ford Motor Company Limited for valuable assistance in preparing this book.

STATON ABBEY

Creek House
St. Osyth
Essex

The high-performance Cortina GT, with a four-headlamp lighting system, special wheels and a matt-black grille

The GXL version, top of the Cortina Mk 3 range for performance and luxury appointments

Contents

1 Getting to know your car

Practical owners usually like to browse through facts and figures, and in any case much of the information given in the following pages will be needed during routine servicing.

Useful as these tables are, however, there is one point to bear in mind: car design is never static and modifications are often made during the product run of a particular model, which may affect some of the figures in the tables. If in doubt, you will usually find your Ford dealer ready to give friendly advice.

ENGINE SPECIFICATION

All models: 4-cylinder, in-line

Model	Capacity	Cylinder Bore	Piston Stroke	Compression Ratio	Power Output (gross Din PS)
1300 (push-rod)	1,298 c.c. (79·2 cu in.)	80·98 mm (3·188 in.)	62·99 mm (2·480 in.)	9·0:1	57 b.h.p. at 5,500 r.p.m.
1600 (push-rod)	1,599 c.c. (97·6 cu in.)	80·98 mm (3·188 in.)	77·62 mm (3·056 in.)	9·0:1	68 b.h.p. at 5,200 r.p.m.
1600GT (o.h.c.)	1,593 c.c. (97·21 cu in.)	87·65 mm (3·45 in.)	66 mm (2·60 in.)	9·2:1	88 b.h.p. at 5,700 r.p.m.
2000 (o.h.c.)	1,993 c.c. (121·6 cu in.)	90·8 mm (3·575 in.)	76·95 mm (3·03 in.)	9·2:1	98 b.h.p. at 5,500 r.p.m.

RECOMMENDED GRADES OF PETROL

Minimum octane rating for all models	97–98 octane (4-star rating)

ENGINE MAINTENANCE DETAILS

	Inlet	Exhaust
Valve tappet clearance, hot		
1300 and 1600 (push-rod)	0·010 in. (0·25 mm)	0·020 in. (0·50 mm)
1600GT (o.h.c.), 2000	0·008 in. (0·20 mm)	0·010 in. (0·25 mm)
Contact-breaker gap		
Autolite (Ford)	0·025 in (0·64 mm)	
Bosch	0·016–0·020 in. (0·40–0·50 mm)	
Sparking plugs		
1300 and 1600 (push-rod)	Autolite AG 22A (14 mm)	
1600GT (o.h.c.), 2000	Autolite BF 32 (18 mm)	

ENGINE MAINTENANCE DETAILS *(contd.)*

Sparking-plug gap, all models	0·025 in. (0·64 mm)
Firing order	
1300 and 1600 (push-rod)	1, 2, 4, 3
1600GT (o.h.c.), 2000	1, 3, 4, 2
Oil pressure, all models	35–40 lb/sq in. (2·5–2·8 kg/cm^2)
Static ignition timing	
2000	4° B.T.D.C.
All other models	6° B.T.D.C.
Idling speed	
1300 and 1600 (push-rod)	700–800 r.p.m.
All other models	780–820 r.p.m.

CAPACITIES (approx.)

	Imp gal	Litres
Fuel tank	12	54
	Imp pints	*Litres*
Engine sump oil (including filter and oilways)	6	3·5
Gearbox, manual		
1300, 1600, 1600GT	1½	0·9
2000	2½	1·4
Gearbox, automatic	11¼	6·4
Rear axle		
1300, 1600, 1600GT	1¾	1·0
2000	2	1·1
Cooling system (with heater)		
1300	10¼	5·8
1600 and 1600GT	11¼–11½	6·3–6·5
2000	12½	7·1
Heater capacity	1½	0·78

FUEL SYSTEM

Fuel pump
   Type
    Mechanical, driven from eccentric on camshaft or auxiliary shaft.

   Delivery pressure
   Push-rod engines   3·5–5·0 lb/sq in. (0·25–0·35 kg/cm^2)
   o.h.c. engines   3·75–5·0 lb/sq in. (0·26–0·35 kg/cm^2)

Carburettor
   1300 and 1600 (push-rod)   Ford GPD, single-venturi downdraught
   1600GT and 2000   Dual-barrel Weber downdraught, differential throttle opening.
   Standard jet settings should not be changed without consulting a Ford dealer

RECOMMENDED LUBRICANTS AND FLUIDS

Engine
Climatic temperature—
up to —18°C (0°F)   5W/20 or 5W/30
—18°C to 0°C (0°F to 32°F)   10W, 10W/30 or 10W/40
0°C to 32°C (32°F to 90°F)   20W/20, 20W/30, 20W/40, 20W/50, 10W/30, 10W/40 or
   (all temperate climates)   10W/50.
Over 32° (90°F)   40, 20W/40 or 20W/50.

Gearbox   SAE 80 gear oil

Automatic transmission   M–2C33F, from Ford dealers.

Rear axle   SAE 90 EP hypoid gear oil.

Steering gear   SAE 90 EP hypoid gear oil.

Front wheel bearings   Lithium-base grease EMIC–3

Generator   Engine oil.

Distributor   Engine oil and lithium-base grease—see pages 46–7.

General-purpose grease   Lithium-base grease with molybdenum disulphide.

Brake fluid reservoir   ESEA–M6C–1001A (or latest recommendation by the
                                                    Ford Motor Company).

ELECTRICAL SYSTEM

Type	Negative earth
Voltage	12 volt
Battery capacity	38 amp/hr

COOLING SYSTEM

Type   Pressurized, circulation by engine-driven pump.

Radiator filler cap pressure   13 lb/sq in. (0·91 kg/cm^2).

Thermostat
Type   Wax capsule
Opening temperature   85–89°C (185–192°F)   add ±3°C (5·4°F) to these
Fully-open temperature   99–102°C (210–216°F) figures for used thermostats.

STEERING

The steering geometry is set during assembly and
cannot be adjusted, except for front-wheel
alignment

Front-wheel alignment, service setting—
Toe-in $\frac{5}{32}$ in. (3·97 mm)
Acceptable tolerance range   0–$\frac{1}{4}$ in. (0–6·3 mm)

DIMENSIONS AND WEIGHTS (approx.)

Overall length	14 ft 0 in. (4·267 m)
Overall width	5 ft 7 in. (1·703 m)
Overall height	4 ft 4 in. (1·321 m)
Ground Clearance	5 in. (127 mm)
Turning circle, between kerbs	33½ ft (10·605 m)

Weights

1300 and 1600 saloons	19 cwt (965 kg)
1300 and 1600 estate cars	20½–21 cwt (1,041–1,067 kg)
1600GT saloon	19¾ cwt (1,003 kg)
2000 saloon	20 cwt (1,016 kg)
2000 estate car	21½ cwt (1,092 kg)

Add approx. ½ cwt (25 kg) where automatic transmission is fitted

RECOMMENDED COLD TYRE PRESSURES

Pressures in lb/sq in. (kg/sq cm) Tyre Size	Normal Laden[1] Front	Rear	Fully Laden[2] Front	Rear
Saloon				
5·60–13 4PR	26 (1·8)	26 (1·8)	27 (1·9)	30 (2·1)
6·00–13 4PR	24 (1·7)	24 (1·7)	24 (1·7)	30 (2·1)
6·45–13 4PR	24 (1·7)	24 (1·7)	27 (1·9)	30 (2·1)
6·45–S13 4PR	27 (1·9)	27 (1·9)	27 (1·9)	34 (2·4)
6·95–S13 4PR	27 (1·9)	27 (1·9)	27 (1·9)	34 (2·4)
165 SR13	23 (1·6)	20 (1·4)	27 (1·9)	34 (2·4)
175 SR13	20 (1·4)	20 (1·4)	27 (1·9)	34 (2·4)
185/70 HR13	22 (1·5)	20 (1·4)	27 (1·9)	34 (2·4)
Estate Car				
6·00–13 6PR	24 (1·7)	24 (1·7)	27 (1·9)	36 (2·5)
6·45–13 6PR	24 (1·7)	24 (1·7)	27 (1·9)	36 (2·5)
6·45–S13 6PR	27 (1·9)	27 (1·9)	27 (1·9)	40 (2·8)
6·95–S13 4PR	27 (1·9)	27 (1·9)	27 (1·9)	34 (2·4)
165 SR13	24 (1·7)	27 (1·9)	27 (1·9)	36 (2·5)
175 SR13	24 (1·7)	27 (1·9)	27 (1·9)	34 (2·4)
185/70 HR13	27 (1·9)	27 (1·9)	27 (1·9)	36 (2·5)
Heavy Duty Estate 175 SR13 reinforced	24 (1·7)	27 (1·9)	27 (1·9)	43 (3·0)

[1] Normal laden tyre pressures apply when vehicle is loaded with up to 3 persons.
[2] Fully laden tyre pressures apply when vehicle is loaded in excess of the normal laden condition as described above.

TORQUE-WRENCH SETTINGS

As emphasized in other chapters, it is advisable to tighten some of the more important nuts and bolts to a specified torque figure, expressed in lb ft and kg m, in order to obtain the correct tightness without risking over-stressing a bolt or nut or distorting a part. Torque-wrench settings for the more critical components dealt with during routine maintenance are given on page 5.

Engine

	Tightening Torque lb ft (kg m)
Cylinder-head bolts—all engines	65–70 (9–9·7)
Main-bearing cap bolts—all engines	65–70 (9–9·7)
Connecting-rod big end—all engines	30–35 (4·1–4·8)
Flywheel-to-crankshaft bolts	
push-rod engines	50–55 (6·9–7·6)
o.h.c. engines	47–51 (6·5–7)
Rocker shaft—push-rod engines	17–22 (2·35–3)
Rocker cover bolts—o.h.c. engines	
1st stage	3·5–5 (0·5–0·7), 1st to 6th bolt
2nd stage	1·5–2 (0·2–0·25), 7th and 8th bolt
3rd stage	3·5–5 (0·5–0·7), 9th and 10th bolt
4th stage	3·5–5 (0·5–0·7), 7th and 8th bolt
Sparking plugs	
push-rod engines	22–29 (3–4)
	14·5–20 (2–2·8)

Suspension, Brakes and Wheels

Wheel nuts	50–65 (7–8·9)
Brake calliper to front suspension unit	45–47 (6·22–6·91)
Front brake disc to hub	30–33 (4·2–4·7)
Axle shaft bearing retainer bolts	15–18 (2·1–2·4)
*Radius arms to axle and body	42–50 (5·8–6·9)
*Coil spring to bottom plate	28–35 (3·9–4·8)

*These items to be tightened with the components in the kerb weight position, i.e. the car must be resting on its wheels.

2 Servicing for beginners

So you have a practical turn of mind, and would like to carry out as much routine maintenance and servicing of your car as possible? One must draw the line somewhere, of course, and the sort of jobs that you should tackle will depend on your experience and on the tools and equipment at your disposal. Routine adjustments and servicing should be well within your scope, even if you are a novice. As you gain experience, you should be able to cope with the more advanced work described in this book.

The cost of a basic tool kit will eventually be more than offset by savings in garage labour charges, which usually form the largest part of servicing and repair bills nowadays; but a bigger dividend is the knowledge that no items have been scamped or overlooked. There is a good chance, too, of discovering any trouble at an early stage, before it can result in an expensive repair or a roadside breakdown.

The Tools You Will Need. No job can be done properly without the right tools. You will probably have to buy a few items to supplement the collection of screwdrivers, pliers and so forth that the average home handyman accumulates over a period of years.

Metric screw threads are extensively used on these cars and nuts and bolts on this type call for the use of metric (sometimes called MM) spanner sizes. The 1300 and 1600 engines have mostly "Unified" nuts and bolts, measured across the flats in fractions of an inch. The spanners for these are usually termed AF sizes. It would be advisable to purchase a set of good-quality ring or socket spanners in metric and AF sizes, to supplement the usual open-jawed spanners. If you can afford an extension drive and, possibly, a ratchet handle, so much the better.

Items such as a torque-indicating wrench, a vacuum gauge and an engine compression gauge are desirable (a torque wrench is a "must" if you do any overhauls or repairs), but these can wait until you are ready to tackle more ambitious work.

There is no need to pay top prices for tools which will be used only occasionally in the home garage, but avoid very cheap tool sets which are simply marked "Foreign." These are usually of very poor quality and have a short life. Tools from West Germany and Spain, however, are normally very good value for money.

BASIC TOOL KIT

The following are essential items for routine servicing, which can be added to as more ambitious work is undertaken. Special service tools (when needed—and fortunately this does not apply to most of the jobs covered by this book) can sometimes be hired from a local Ford dealer:

Set of open-ended or ring, or combination spanners,
AF and Metric sizes.
Set of socket spanners, with extension, in same size range
Selection of screwdrivers, including two sizes for cross-head screws
Large and small adjustable spanner
Self-locking adjustable spanner (Mole wrench type)
Side-cutting and pointed-nose 6 in. pliers
Set of feeler gauges
Sparking plug gap-setting tool
Tyre-pressure gauge
Tyre tread-depth gauge
Engineer's hammer (ball pane)
Fine carborundum stone
Wire brush
Inspection lamp

A good tyre-pressure gauge is essential. Garage pressure gauges are not always as accurate as they should be; and pressures should always be checked with the tyres *cold*, which is obviously impossible if the car has to be driven to a garage or if pressures are checked during the course of a journey. Take a tip from rally and competition drivers and spend a little more on a dial-type gauge, which gives clearer readings than the telescopic type.

A tyre tread-depth gauge is an inexpensive item which will enable you to keep a check on the rate of wear of the tyres and will also indicate when they are due for replacement. The official regulation in Britain calls for 1 mm of tread over three-quarters of the width of the tread pattern, around the complete circumference of the tyre, but it is much safer to change the tyres when the treads are worn down to a depth of 2 mm.

An electrical drill is, perhaps, something of a luxury, but the way in which it can speed-up a surprisingly large number of jobs, particularly if it is provided with the usual range of accessories, such as wire brushes for decarbonizing the cylinder head, a grindstone and a lambswool polishing mop, renders it a really worthwhile investment for an owner who carries out any appreciable amount of work.

Turning the Engine when Making Adjustments. The fact that modern engines are not provided with starting handles makes it difficult to rotate the crankshaft while setting the valve clearances, adjusting the gap between the contact-breaker points or checking the ignition timing.

The most usual method when a manual gearbox is fitted is to remove the sparking plugs (to relieve the compression in the cylinders), engage top gear and then push the car backwards or forwards.

It is sometimes possible to turn the engine by pulling on the fan blades (taking great care not to distort them), while some owners resort to operating the starting motor for a second or so at a time, in the hope of obtaining the correct setting on a hit-and-miss principle.

The real answer to the problem, however, is to invest in an ingenious device known as the Pronto 80 remote control, which is obtainable from garages and accessory shops, or from Positune Ltd., 1–5 Fowler Road, Hainault, Essex. When this is connected-up to the battery and starter solenoid switch, the engine can be "inched" round at the slowest possible speed, making precise adjustment an easy matter.

The device is not expensive and if you intend to carry out home maintenance as a regular rule, it will soon repay its cost, as it can also be used for a number of other jobs, among which are setting the basic ignition timing, checking the actual firing point of the engine and checking the condition of the starter ring gear.

Workbench and Storage. A workbench will be needed for any jobs that are done on components that have been removed from the car, but it is quite possible to make do with a stout kitchen table, which can often be picked up for a few shillings at an auction. If any but elementary servicing is carried out, a vice will be needed. This can often be obtained quite cheaply from a shop which deals in Ministry surplus equipment.

It is much more economical to purchase oil in bulk—say in gallon rather than in pint or quart tins—and a five-gallon drum works out even more cheaply. A wooden stand can be made up to take the drum and a draw-off tap can be purchased to replace the screwed plug in the side of the drum. Needless to say, when fitting the tap the drum should be laid on its side, with the screwed plug uppermost.

Working Beneath the Car. If an inspection pit is not available, a pair of drive-on wheel ramps will also be needed. A cheaper alternative is a pair of adjustable axle stands. These have the advantage of leaving the wheel free to rotate. On the other hand, it takes only a minute or two to drive the front or rear wheels on to a pair of ramps, whereas both sides of the car must be jacked-up to allow stands to be used.

For obvious reasons, ramps or axle-stands which lift only one end of the car must not be used when checking the oil-levels.

Finally, never be tempted to work beneath the car when it is supported only by the jack or by an insecure pile of bricks.

3 Planning do-it-yourself maintenance

Apart from the "first service," which is carried out free by a Ford dealer after the first 600 miles (1,000 km) have been covered, the official Cortina service schedule is based on the mileage or time intervals given in the accompanying home maintenance scheme.

This broadly follows the official maintenance schedule, but some additional jobs that are within the scope of the practical owner have been included. It will be noticed that with a new Cortina, it is advisable to carry out a 6,000-mile check after the first 3,000 miles have been covered, and then to follow the normal schedule. If you have bought a used car, give it a 30,000-mile check immediately, to make sure that all is well. Some car dealers do this as a matter of course during pre-sale preparation of used cars, but most seem to consider that a 6,000-mile service is adequate.

If you cover a relatively small mileage during the year, work to the time intervals given in the schedule, without waiting for the speedometer reading to reach the specified mileages. If you cover, say, only 6,000 miles in a year, there is a risk of trouble developing which could become serious if it were not detected in the early stages.

It is also advisable to have the car put on a garage hoist at least twice a year, so that a thorough inspection of the underside can be made in reasonable comfort. Look especially for signs of rust developing in the underframe and floor, chafed or rusty brake lines, leaks from the exhaust system, loose nuts and bolts and for signs of accidental damage.

Each item in the home-maintenance schedule has been given a job number, the first part of which indicates the frequency with which the work must be done: W–1 is a weekly job, 6–1 a 6,000-mile service item, and so on. On turning to the page reference, you will find a detailed explanation of the job.

If you are working single-handed at home, however, you will quickly discover that the main drawback of a rigid schedule is the time factor. The 6,000-mile service, for example, is likely to take up the better part of a week-end. There is a lot to be said for spreading the load as much as possible.

Draw up a maintenance chart which will allow two or three jobs to be

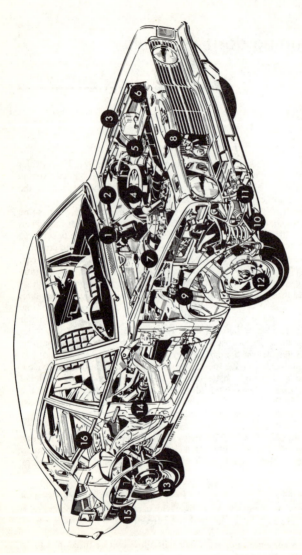

Fig. 1. Some features of the Cortina which affect maintenance and servicing

1, windscreen wiper; 2, interior heater; 3, windscreen washer reservoir; 4, air cleaner; 5, radiator filler cap; 6, battery; 7, brake servo and fluid reservoir; 8, radiator and fan; 9, propellor-shaft universal joint; 10, coil-spring front suspension; 11, rack-and-pinion steering gear; 12, front-wheel disc brake; 13, rear-wheel drum brake; 14, rear axle; 15, petrol tank; 16, spare wheel, beneath boot floor

done comfortably in an hour or so once a week. How this is arranged will depend, of course, on the average weekly mileage.

There is no need to adhere too rigidly to the specified mileage intervals. A few hundred miles on either side are not critical. In any case, an enthusiastic owner usually spends a good deal of time at weekends or in the evenings on tuning and adjustments—or "profitable tinkering," as it has been aptly termed.

PLANNED HOME MAINTENANCE

Job Number		Page Number

Every 250 miles (400 km) or weekly

W–1	*Engine.* Check oil level and top-up if necessary (check daily if engine is worn and also when refilling with fuel on a long run)	17
W–2	*Radiator.* Check water level when cold and top-up if necessary. . .	37
W–3	*Wheels and Tyres.* Check tyre pressures *when cold*. Watch for cuts and signs of uneven wear. Check tightness of wheel nuts	87–8
W–4	*Battery.* Check level of liquid in cells	90
W–5	*Windscreen Washer Reservoir.* Check level of fluid	—
W–6	*Brake Fluid Reservoir.* Check level of fluid (this is a precautionary check only—topping-up should be required only at long intervals, unless a leak has developed in the system)	74

After the first 3,000 miles (5,000 km) or first 3 months with a new car

General Check. Carry out a full 6,000-mile service—see below

Every 6,000 miles (10,000 km) or every 6 months

Carry out jobs W–1 to W–6 and following additional work

6–1	*Engine Lubrication.* Drain oil and refill sump	18
6–2	*Engine.* Renew oil filter element	18
6–3	*Engine.* Check valve clearances. Adjust if necessary . . .	20
6–4	*Engine.* Check oil filler cap. Service crankcase breather valve . .	22
6–5	*Cooling System.* Check condition of hoses, and for leaks when engine is running fast	39
6–6	*Fan and Generator Driving Belt.* Check belt tension. Adjust if necessary .	39
6–7	*Carburettor Air-cleaner.* Check condition of element . . .	65
6–8	*Carburettor.* Check slow-running adjustments. Lubricate accelerator cable and adjust if necessary	58
6–9	*Exhaust System.* Check for tightness of manifold and clamp bolts, gas leakages, corroded pipes and silencers, and condition of hangers and insulators .	—
6–10	*Sparking Plugs.* Clean; check and reset gaps. Renew if necessary . .	44
6–11	*Ignition Distributor.* Lubricate distributor. Clean or renew contact points and adjust gap. Clean distributor rotor and cap. . . 46, 47, 50
6–12	*Ignition System.* Check ignition timing. Preferably have system checked with electronic test-tune equipment	52–6
6–13	*Clutch.* Check free movement of pedal. Adjust if necessary . .	68
6–14	*Gearbox or Automatic Transmission.* Check oil level	70
6–15	*Rear Axle.* Check oil level	72
6–16	*Brakes—Preventive Check.* Check fluid level in reservoir. Remove rear brake drums. Check thickness of linings. Check operating cylinders for leakage. Blow out dust. Check thickness of front brake friction pads. Check handbrake adjustment. Check flexible hoses for chafing and steel pipes for chafing and rusting	74–5
6–17	*Steering Gear and Front Suspension.* Check bellows or rack-and-pinion unit for splits, or leakage. Check steering and suspension joints for damaged grease-retaining gaiters and for wear	81–3
6–18	*Shock Absorbers (Dampers).* Check for signs of fluid leakage. Test efficiency by bouncing each corner of car.	84

PLANNED HOME MAINTENANCE (contd.)

Job Number		Page Number

6–19 *Wheels.* Remove road wheels, wash and examine for possible damage, change from side to side at front and rear when refitting. Grease wheel studs. Have wheel balance checked 83

6–20 *Tyres.* Inspect tyre treads. Check tread depth with tyre tread gauge. If unevenly worn, have wheel alignment checked. Check sidewalls for cuts and other damage. Prise out embedded flints 87–8

6–21 *Electrical System.* Check battery acid level. Clean and tighten terminals. Check operation of charging system, starter motor, lights and instruments . 89–104

6–22 *Dynamo.* Lubricate end bearing. 93

6–23 *Oil-can Lubrication.* Apply a few drops of oil to throttle linkage, handbrake linkage, door, boot and bonnet locks and hinges . . . . . —

6–24 *Bodywork.* Check for chips and scratches in paintwork. Check that drain holes are clear, and that heater box drain is not clogged . . . . . —

Every 12,000 miles (20,000 km) or every 12 months

Carry out the 6,000-mile service and following additional work

12–1 *Carburettor.* Clean float chamber and jets. Adjust idling speed and mixture strength 58–65

12–2 *Carburettor Air-cleaner.* Renew element 65

12–3 *Petrol Filters.* Clean fuel pump filter. Renew in-line fuel filter . . . 67

12–4 *Front Wheel Bearings.* Check for leakage of grease, excessive end-play and noise from bearings when wheel is rotated 85

12–5 *Steering and Front Suspension.* Have front-wheel alignment and steering geometry checked by dealer

12–6 *Cooling System.* De-scale, flush and refill. Check operation of thermostat (this should be a regular autumn service) 40–2

12–7 *Propellor Shafts.* Check condition of universal joints and tightness of coupling bolts 71

12–8 *Road Test.* Give car a thorough road test (including operation of automatic transmission, when fitted) and carry out any adjustments required. If possible have final check made with electronic test-tune equipment and check compression in cylinders. After test, check for oil, fuel, fluid or grease leaks at all plugs, flanges, joints and unions . . . . —

Every 30,000 miles (50,000 km) or 18 months

Carry out the 6,000 and 12,000-mile services and the following additional work

30–1 *Front-wheel Hubs.* Dismantle, clean out grease and lubricate with fresh grease. Re-set end-float on bearings 85

30–2 *Front Suspension.* Lubricate ball joints 86

Every 40,000 miles (65,000 km) or every 3 years

Carry out the previous services and the following additional work

40–1 *Dynamo.* Check condition of brushes and commutator 93

40–2 *Starter Motor.* Check condition of brushes, commutator and pinion drive assembly 95

40–3 *Speedometer Cable.* Lubricate inner cable with grease . . . . —

40–4 *Braking System.* Renew all flexible hoses and rubber seals in system. Refill system with fresh fluid (consult your Ford dealer about this work) 73

4 The engine

The engines fitted to cars manufactured in Great Britain are of two basic types. First there are the 1300 and 1600 designs. These are push-rod-operated overhead-valve units, already familiar in the Escort and Capri, but uprated for the Cortina to give slightly improved power-output and torque, by revised valve timing, a better inlet manifold design, larger valve ports and different carburettor jets and ignition settings.

Secondly, we have the 1600GT and the 2000 engines, which are new designs incorporating single overhead camshafts, driven by cogged belts. As a matter of interest, a 1,300 c.c. version of this engine is available in the German equivalent to the Cortina (the Taunus) and the 2,000 c.c. engine is also used in an American "subcompact" car, the Ford Pinto.

The 1300 and 1600 Engines. The push-rod-operated engines are of the Heron-head, cross-flow type. Translated into non-technical terms, this means that the combustion chambers are formed in the piston crowns instead of in the cylinder head, and the inlet and exhaust manifolds are on opposite sides of the engine.

The standard arrangement is for the push-rod-operated overhead valves to work in guides drilled directly in the cylinder head, although in some cases inserted valve guides are fitted. When the guides become worn, valves which have oversize stems can be fitted, but reaming the worn guides to provide the correct fit would normally be a job for a Ford dealer. If inserted guides are used, these can also be reamed or new guides can be pressed in.

An interesting feature is that the valve spring caps are retained by tapered collets which locate in grooves in the valve stems but do not grip the stems tightly. The object is to allow the valves to rotate during operation, thus giving a longer life before refacing or renewal becomes necessary.

The cast-iron crankshaft runs in five large-diameter thin-shell, steel-backed main bearings. The forged-steel H-section connecting rods also have steel-backed thin-shell bearings. Steel-backed bronze bushes are used for the little-end bearings. The piston pins are fully floating and are retained in position by circlips in grooves in the piston bosses.

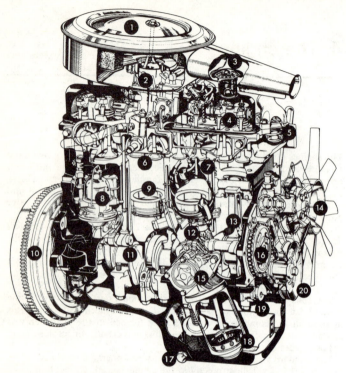

Fig. 2. The 1300 and 1600 push-rod engine

1, *air cleaner*; 2, *carburettor*; 3, *oil filler*; 4, *push-rod overhead valve gear*; 5, *cooling system thermostat*; 6, *valves*; 7, *ignition distributor*; 8, *petrol pump*; 9, *combustion chamber in piston crown*; 10, *flywheel and starter ring gear*; 11, *crankshaft*; 12, *distributor and oil-pump driving gears*; 13, *connecting rod*; 14, *cooling fan*; 15, *oil pump*; 16, *camshaft chain wheel*; 17, *oil-sump drain plug*; 18, *oil filter*; 19, *camshaft chain tensioner*; 20, *crankshaft pulley*

The 1600GT and 2000 Engines. The overhead-camshaft engines are new designs which incorporate a number of interesting features, such as a cogged-belt drive for the single overhead camshaft. The cams operate the valves through cam followers, which pivot on adjustable ball-ended studs, enabling the valve clearances to be set quickly and accurately.

"Mousetrap" anti-rattle springs are fitted at the pivoted ends of the cam followers. As with the push-rod engines, the valves work directly in guides machined in the cylinder head.

The slack in the camshaft belt is taken up by a jockey pulley, and obtaining the correct tension is simplicity itself. It is necessary only to slacken a bolt which locks the plate which carries the pulley, allowing a strong spring to move the plate and the pulley towards the belt. The locking bolt is then retightened and no further adjustment should be needed until the belt is next removed—in the course of a top-overhaul, for example.

Judging by the experience of other manufacturers that have used this type of drive, the cogged belt which is reinforced with glassfibre, can be expected to have a very long life. Unless it is accidentally damaged, it

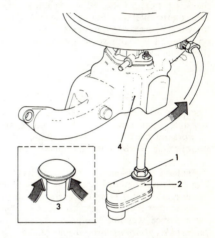

Fig. 3. The crankcase ventilation system consists of a ventilation valve, 1, and an oil separator, 2. Air enters the oil filler cap, 3. The ventilation valve is connected to the inlet manifold, 4

should certainly last between major engine overhauls and the Ford Company make no stipulation regarding its renewal at any specified mileage.

The belt also drives an auxiliary shaft, set low down in the cylinder block, which in turn drives the ignition distributor, oil pump and petrol pump.

Unlike the push-rod engines. the combustion chambers are formed in the cylinder head and flat-top pistons are used. The five-bearing crankshaft and the connecting rods, which have thin-shell steel-backed bearings, are also conventional in design, except for the fact that no separate locking devices are used on the bearing nuts and bolts. The contact faces of the nuts or bolts are specially formed to lock against the bearing caps.

The piston pins are a freeze-fit in the connecting rod eyes, which must be heated to the correct temperature when new pins are fitted. This is, therefore, normally a job for a Ford dealer. The pistons and piston pins are precisely matched to each other and must be removed as assemblies.

Engine Ventilation. Good "ventilation" of the interior of the engine is essential to prevent fumes being drawn into the car, and to reduce the formation of sludge inside the crankcase and valve cover. A positive ventilation system is therefore fitted as standard to all engines. The fumes are drawn from the crankcase into the inlet manifold through an oil separator and an emission control valve, fitted into a grommet on top of the separator and connected by a tube to the manifold. Fresh air enters through a breather incorporated in the oil filler cap.

A positive flow of air through the engine is thus created, but the risk of the idling mixture strength being diluted by an excessive amount of air entering the inlet manifold is prevented by the emission valve just referred to, which opens when the engine is running at normal speeds. As explained on pages 58–9, if this valve is neglected, idling will be unsatisfactory and the engine may stall.

ROUTINE ENGINE MAINTENANCE

The jobs described in this chapter are those listed in the maintenance schedule. Engine maintenance, of course, also includes a certain amount of work on the cooling system, ignition system and the carburettor and petrol pump. These jobs are dealt with in Chapter 5, 6 and 7.

Engine Lubrication. The engine oil has been aptly described as the life-blood of the engine. It therefore pays to use a first-class lubricant. A "multigrade" oil is best. The correct grades are given on page 3.

Remember that the intervals between oil changes recommended in the maintenance schedule *apply only when a multigrade oil is used, under favourable conditions.* More frequent changes are advisable when most of the driving is done in cold weather, or when the car is used frequently for short runs and frequent starts are made from cold. At the other extreme, hot, dusty conditions will also cause rapid deterioration of the oil.

In such cases it is best to change the oil after 3,000 miles, or, in extreme cases, as frequently as every 1,000 miles.

Oil Pressure. When an oil-pressure gauge is not provided, the oil-pressure warning lamp in the instrument panel will glow if the oil pressure should fall below a safe minimum figure. The lamp should, of course, light-up when the ignition is first switched on, but should be extinguished when the engine is running. If the lamp does not light-up, or does not go out when the engine is running, it is possible that the switch on the cylinder block, which is operated by the oil pressure, is faulty. Either fit a replacement switch, or ask a garage to check the oil pressure by temporarily connecting a gauge to the switch union.

The correct oil pressure is given in Chapter 1. If the pressure is appreciably below this figure at normal speeds in top gear, with the engine thoroughly warmed-up, investigation is called for. Running the engine with too low a pressure can result in expensive damage to the crankshaft, main and connecting-rod bearings and other components.

Fortunately the oil pump is seldom at fault, except when the engine has covered a very large mileage, and the pick-up filter in the sump should not need cleaning between engine overhauls. The oil-pressure relief valve is a possible culprit, however. This valve relieves the excessive pressure that would otherwise build-up when the pump attempts to force the oil through the oilways after the engine is started from cold. If it sticks open, the oil pressure will be too low when the oil has warmed-up and flows freely.

The valve is incorporated in the oil pump and cannot be checked without removing the pump. It consists of a spring-loaded piston, and if it gives trouble the simplest cure is to fit a reconditioned pump. Consult your Ford dealer about this. In the case of the overhead-camshaft engine, the pump is in the engine sump, and to take this off, the engine must be removed.

If satisfactory pressure is not restored when the above points have been attended to, the crankshaft and connecting-rod-bearings are probably worn, calling for a partial or complete overhaul as described in Chapter 13.

Having dealt with some of the general aspects of engine lubrication, we can now consider in more detail the lubrication jobs that are specified in the home-servicing scheme.

W-1: Checking the Engine Oil Level

1 Switch off the engine and wait for several minutes before taking a reading with the dipstick.

2 Remove the dipstick and wipe it with a clean cloth.

3 Replace the dipstick to its full depth, withdraw it and note the level. If necessary, add oil to bring the level to the high mark.

Special Notes

The oil level should be checked only when the car is standing on level ground. Always allow a few minutes for the oil to drain into the sump after the engine has been switched off, or after oil has been poured into the filler; otherwise a misleadingly low reading will be obtained. It is more economical to keep the oil well topped-up than to allow the level to fall nearly to the low mark on the dipstick before adding more oil, but there is obviously not much sense in adding a pint or so just before the oil is to be changed. Remember that the oil consumption may increase considerably during a fast run in hot weather. Check the level at each petrol stop.

6-1: Changing the Engine Oil

1 Make sure that the engine is thoroughly warmed-up.

2 Place a container which will hold about two gallons (to provide a safety margin) beneath the drain plug and unscrew the plug. Allow the oil to drain until the drips have ceased.

3 Clean the drain plug, check that the copper washer is in good condition and replace the plug. Refill the sump and warm-up the engine.

4 Check for leakage at the drain plug. Re-check the oil-level with the car on level ground (Job No. W-1).

Special Notes

It is best to drain the oil when the car has just come in from a run. New multigrade oil will darken fairly quickly in service, but this merely indicates that the detergent in the oil is doing its job and is keeping the carbon and other particles in suspension.

An old kitchen washing-up bowl will serve as a drain pan, or a two-gallon tin with one side cut out. Allow sufficient time for all the oil to drain completely before replacing the drain plug.

The oil filter element should be changed at every oil change.

6-2: Fitting a New Oil Filter

A full-flow, throw-away type of oil filter is provided, and this must be renewed after it has been in use for 6,000 miles (10,000 km). Carbon, sludge and grit accumulate in the filter, and the element becomes clogged, a safety valve opens in order to maintain adequate oil circulation to the engine—*but this oil will not be filtered.*

To renew the filter:

1 Drain the oil (operation 6–1).

2 Unscrew the filter and discard it.

3 Clean the joint face on the cylinder block and smear the joint ring on the new filter with clean engine oil.

4 Screw the filter into position until it just touches the joint face on the cylinder block. Then screw it in by a further two-thirds of a turn by hand only. *The filter must not be tightened with a spanner.*

Special Notes

The rubber seal tends to stick to the cylinder block and it may be difficult to unscrew. It may be necessary to use a chain-wrench to free it. Altern-atively, drive an old screwdriver through the filter body in order to provide sufficient leverage to break the joint.

Fig. 4. The overhead-camshaft engine of the 1600GT and 2000 models

1, camshaft pulley; 2, oil filler; 3, camshaft; 4, rocking cam follower; 5, valve spring; 6, inlet and exhaust valves; 7, manifold; 8, ignition distributor; 9, generator; 10, cooling fan; 11, camshaft belt tensioner; 12, piston; 13, connecting-rod; 14, flywheel and starter ring gear; 15, pulley driving auxiliary shaft; 16, cogged belt drive; 17 water-pump impeller; 18, distributor driving shaft; 19, crankshaft; 20, crankshaft vee-pulley; 21, oil pump; 22, petrol pump; 23, oil pick-up in sump; 24, oil sump drain plug

6-3: Checking the Valve Tappet Clearances

To ensure that the correct gap exists between the tip of each valve and the rocker that operates it, check the valves at 5,000-mile intervals.

The effective opening period of the valve will be changed if the clearance becomes too small. If no clearance exists, the valve will be held off its

Fig. 5. Adjusting the valve clearances on 1300 and 1600 push-rod engines. After slackening the lock-nut, the adjusting screw, 1, is turned while the gap is checked with the feeler gauge, 2. The clearance must not be adjusted when the rocker is partly depressed, as at 3

seating, which will cause rapid burning of the valve face and the seating in the cylinder head, and will lead, of course, to loss of compression in that cylinder. Too large a clearance will restrict the opening of the valve and the time that it is off its seating.

The correct tappet clearances are given in Chapter 1. They must be measured with the engine hot except, of course, after an engine overhaul, when they should be set during assembly and re-checked after the engine has been run and has reached its normal temperature. *Never check the clearances when the engine is warm*, as misleading results will be obtained.

To check and adjust the clearances on push-rod engines:

1 Remove the rocker cover, being careful not to damage the gasket. If this is found to be brittle or broken, obtain a replacement.

2 It is important that each tappet should be on the base of its cam. This can be ensured by checking two valves while two others are "rocking." This means that both valves are open together, but each will begin to close if the engine is turned away from the top-dead-centre position. Check the clearances in the following sequences:

Valves Rocking	*Valves to Check*
1 (exhaust) and 6 (inlet)	3 (inlet) and 8 (exhaust)
3 (inlet) and 8 (exhaust)	1 (exhaust) and 6 (inlet)
2 (inlet) and 4 (exhaust)	5 (exhaust) and 7 (inlet)
5 (exhaust) and 7 (inlet)	2 (inlet) and 4 (exhaust)

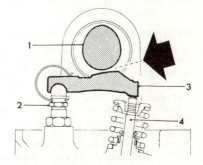

Fig. 6. On overhead-camshaft engines the valve clearance is measured between the cam, 1, and the follower, 3, at the point shown by the arrow. The adjustment is made by turning the pivot, 2. The valve stem is shown at 4

3 Slide a feeler gauge between the end of the rocker and the tip of the valve stem. It should be a light drag fit—not too loose nor too tight.

4 If adjustment is needed, slacken the lock-nut at the push-rod end of the rocker (preferably use a ring spanner, as the edges of the flats on the nut can easily be burred-over by an open-jawed spanner). Turn the adjusting-screw with a screwdriver until the correct clearance is obtained and hold it in this position while tightening the lock-nut.

5 Re-check the clearance, which will probably have altered during the first attempt at tightening the lock-nut.

6 Replace the valve rocker cover. Tighten the screws evenly and make sure that the gasket is compressed by the cover when the screws are tightened down onto the shoulders of their shanks. If this is not the case, it will be necessary to fit a new gasket.

To check and adjust the clearances on the 1600GT and 2000 (overhead-camshaft) engines:

On these engines, as explained on page 14, each rocker pivots on a hemispherical seating on an adjustable stud. To adjust the valve clearance, therefore, it is necessary only to slacken the lock-nut and to screw the stud downwards to increase the clearance or upwards to decrease it.

Since it can be seen when each cam is pointing straight upwards, checking the clearance between the base of the cam and the cam follower presents no difficulty. The instruction given to check the clearances with pairs of valves rocking, which is given in some Cortina Owner Handbooks, *does not apply to the overhead-camshaft engines*.

Special Notes

As a starting handle is not provided, the most convenient method of rotating the engine is to remove the sparking plugs to relieve the compression and turn the crankshaft by engaging top gear and moving the car backwards and forwards.

6-4: Cleaning the Engine Breather Valve

As described on page 16, the engines are fitted with a semi-sealed crankcase ventilation system, in which the flow of air into the inlet manifold is regulated by a breather valve which fits into a grommet in the top of the oil separator, which is a push-fit in the crankcase, to the rear of the carburettor.

In time, the valve tends to become clogged by carbon and oily sludge. While it is unlikely that the hose connecting it to the inlet manifold will be badly restricted, except after a considerable mileage, both the hose and the valve should be inspected and cleaned at 6,000-mile intervals.

If the valve sticks in the closed position, all the fumes will not be drawn out of the crankcase when the engine is running at normal speeds. If it sticks open, too much air will by-pass the plunger when the engine is idling, the idling mixture will be weakened and the engine may stall. And thirdly, if the bleed holes in the valve, which permit the correct amount of air to enter the manifold when the engine is idling and the valve is closed, become clogged-up, the idling mixture strength will be too rich and the engine will have a slow and lumpy tick-over, again with the possibility of stalling.

It is a simple matter to remove the valve and clean the parts with methylated spirits. It can be dismantled by removing the circlip from the end which plugs into the oil separator. When reassembling the valve, the smaller-diameter coils on the spring must face the flange of the plunger.

When the valve is cleaned, the oil filler cap, which contains a gauze filter element, should also be swilled in paraffin. You will notice that if this cap is removed when the engine is idling, the engine will speed-up. This is quite normal, and shows that the valve is operating properly.

DECARBONIZING AND TOP-OVERHAUL

Modern oils and fuels leave only light deposits of carbon in the combustion chambers and on the valves and piston crowns, but removal of the cylinder head, cleaning-off the carbon and restoring a good seal between the valves and their seatings, is still usually referred to as "decarbonizing" the engine.

It is more correct to call this a "top-overhaul," especially as the need for the work depends largely on the condition of the valves. The exhaust valves are the most liable to become pitted or burnt and often need refacing or replacement after a life of about 15,000–20,000 miles (24,000–32,000 km). The symptoms that all is not well are a gradual loss of power, "pinking" or detonation when the engine is under load, and, possibly, difficulty in starting.

Similar symptoms can, of course, be caused by carburation or ignition faults, so to discover where the trouble lies, check the compression in each cylinder with a special compression gauge, or get a garage to do this for you. The readings should be equal, to within a few pounds per square inch, on all cylinders. If a low reading is obtained on one or more, the most likely cause is burnt or pitted valve faces. Leakage of gases past the piston rings cannot, of course, be ruled out, but this fault will normally be accompanied by excessive oil consumption.

Tools and Spares Required. Before starting a top overhaul, get together the usual tools used for routine maintenance, plus the following additional tools and spares.

Valve-spring compressor. It may be possible to hire this from a local garage. If the special Ford valve spring compressor recommended for the overhead-camshaft engines is used, it will be necessary also to use the special valve retainer, which screws into the sparking-plug hole and retains each valve on its seat while the spring is being compressed. A large G-type compressor can be used, however, and this renders the valve retaining tool unnecessary.

Locating studs. Two of these are screwed into the cylinder block in order to position the gasket correctly when fitting the cylinder head.

Torque-indicating wrench. Nowadays this is regarded as essential. This is not a cheap tool, and some mechanics claim that it is not needed, but it is an insurance against trouble caused by incorrect or uneven tightening of vital nuts and bolts.

Suction-cup valve-grinding tool. This is not expensive

Blunt scraper. An old chisel will do.

Wire brush. This is needed to remove carbon. A rotary brush, used with an electric drill, saves a lot of time.

Set of new valve springs. If you carry out the top-overhaul properly, you can anticipate that the car should run for upwards of 20,000 miles (32,000 km) before the head is next due for removal; but "tired" valve springs can undo all the careful work put into the overhaul.

Set of rubber oil seals for valve stems. These must be renewed; otherwise excessive oil consumption can be expected.

Set of gaskets and hoses. The modest cost of the gaskets is an insurance

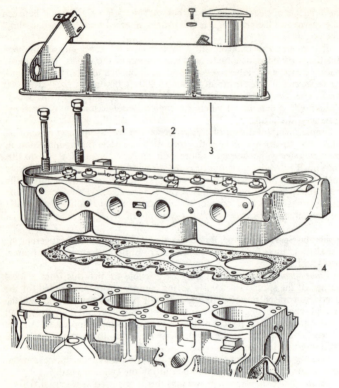

Fig. 7. The cylinder head of a 1300 or 1600 push-rod engine
1, *cylinder-head retaining bolt;* 2, *cylinder head;* 3, *valve cover;* 4, *cylinder-head gasket*

against water, gas or oil leakages after the engine has been reassembled, which would, of course, mean that the parts would again have to be dismantled and reassembled. It is also advisable to renew the water hoses.

Other essentials: a small tin of valve-grinding paste; a plentiful supply of clean rags, free from fluff; a selection of tins or jars in which small items can be left to soak in paraffin pending reassembly; and a dish or tray in which to swill the parts.

When purchasing the items for a top overhaul, ask the dealer whether he can let you have an old piston ring which will fit the bores; this will be useful when decarbonizing the pistons, as described later.

Removing the Cylinder Head from Push-rod Engines

1 Disconnect the battery and drain the cooling system. If anti-freeze is in use, it is better to discard it and fill-up with new anti-freeze when the engine is reassembled.

2 Remove the carburettor air cleaner.

3 Remove the bolts which secure the thermostat housing, pull the housing to one side and lift out the thermostat for checking.

4 Disconnect the heater hoses, and the vacuum hose from the inlet manifold when servo brakes are fitted. If an automatic transmission is fitted, disconnect the automatic choke hoses.

5 Pull the connector off the temperature gauge sender unit.

6 Detach the exhaust pipe from the manifold and move it clear of the cylinder head.

7 Disconnect the throttle cable and linkage, the choke cable, the fuel pipe and the distributor vacuum pipe from the carburettor. If an automatic transmission is fitted, disconnect the downshift cable.

8 Disconnect the leads from the sparking plugs and take out the plugs. Take off the distributor cap.

9 Unclip the carburettor ventilation pipe from the rocker cover (this is not necessary on all engines) and remove the rocker cover and gasket.

10 Unscrew the rocker shaft bolts progressively and lift off the shaft assembly. Take out the push-rods, giving each a twist to break the suction of the oil in the cam follower at its base, and lay out the rods in the order in which they are removed. Roll each push-rod on a flat surface to check that it is not bent and lay the set of rods out in order, so that each rod can be fitted in its original position when the engine is reassembled. Never allow the rods to be mixed; in service, the ball-ends and cups on the rods become lapped to the tappets and rocker screws with which they mate. Any bent rods must be scrapped.

11 The cylinder head bolts can now be undone progressively in the reverse order to that shown in Fig. 10 and the head can be lifted off. If the sparking plugs have not been removed, do not lay the head face downwards on the bench as this will damage the plugs.

Removing the Cylinder Head from Overhead-camshaft Engines

Removal of the cylinder head from an overhead-camshaft engine is straightforward, the only complication being that the camshaft driving belt must be disengaged from the cogged pulley on the camshaft. As the belt also drives the auxiliary shaft, which in turn drives the ignition distributor (in addition to the oil pump and petrol pump), it will be necessary to reset the valve timing and the ignition timing when the cylinder head is being replaced.

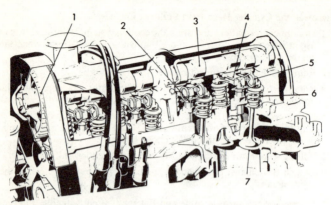

Fig. 8. The valve gear of an overhead-camshaft engine

1, *camshaft driving pulley*; 2, *valve clearance adjuster*; 3, *cam*; 4, *rocking cam follower*; 5, *anti-rattle spring*; 6, *valve spring*; 7, *valve*

It is not necessary to remove the camshaft when carrying out a top-overhaul. If the camshaft bearings are badly worn or the oil seal is leaking, it is best to discuss the job with a Ford dealer, as special tools are required to recondition the various parts.

1 Disconnect the battery earthing strap.

2 Drain the cooling system. Remove the upper radiator hose. Disconnect the wire from the temperature-gauge sender unit.

3 Remove the carburettor air cleaner. Disconnect the accelerator cable.

4 Disconnect the sparking-plug leads and remove the plugs.

5 Detach the exhaust pipe from the manifold.

6 Remove the guard from the toothed-belt drive. Slacken the locking bolt which passes through the slot in the plate on which the belt tensioner is mounted. Pull the tensioner away from the bolt, against the spring pressure and tighten the locking bolt to hold the tensioner clear of the belt. Remove the belt from the camshaft pulley.

7 Unscrew the rocker-cover bolts, disconnect the water hoses, the petrol pipe and the vacuum pipe from the carburettor and inlet manifold. Remove the rocker cover.

8 Unscrew the cylinder-head bolts progressively in the reverse order to that shown in Fig. 10. Lift off the cylinder head, complete with carburettor and manifolds.

Special Notes
The cylinder head, valve gear and manifold assembly is surprisingly heavy

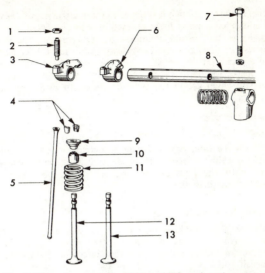

Fig. 9. The valve gear of a 1300 or 1600 push-rod engine

1, *adjusting screw lock-nut*; 2, *valve-clearance adjusting screw*; 3, *rocker*; 4, *collets*; 5, *push-rod*; 6, *rocker*; 7, *retaining bolt*; 8, *rocker shaft*; 9, *valve spring cap*; 10, *valve-stem oil seal*; 11, *valve spring*; 12, *inlet valve*; 13, *exhaust valve*

and an assistant will probably be needed to help to break the joint and lift it clear of the engine compartment.

Special Notes—all Engines

If the water hoses are difficult to remove, they can be cut through with a knife. As mentioned earlier, it is best to fit new hoses on reassembly.

The cylinder-head bolts *must* be slackened progressively, working diagonally from the outside of the head inwards. *This is most important, to avoid distorting the head.*

If the cylinder head does not come away easily, don't attempt to prise it up by inserting a screwdriver or similar tool between the head and the block, as this may damage the machined surfaces. A sharp tap with a wooden mallet, or with a hammer on a block of wood held against the side of the head, should free the joint.

Dismantling the Cylinder Head

If you do not intend to carry out a top-overhaul—for example, if the only reason for removing the cylinder head is to renew a faulty cylinder-head gasket—the combustion chambers can be decarbonized without further dismantling, although it is better to remove the manifolds to allow the inlet and exhaust ports to be cleaned out. In any event, it is best to decarbonize the combustion chambers before removing the valves, to avoid the risk of damaging the valve seatings in the cylinder head.

During a top-overhaul, of course, it will be necessary to remove the valves for inspection and refacing of the valves and seatings, or renewal of any valves which are in too poor condition to justify refacing and refitting them.

To dismantle the cylinder head:

1 Take off the inlet and exhaust manifolds.

2 Dismantle the valve gear and remove the valves, as described below; but if the cylinder head is to be decarbonized, defer removing the valves until the combustion chambers have been cleaned and burnished (see below).

Decarbonizing the Cylinder Head

1 Decarbonize the combustion-chamber faces before removing the valves, to avoid any risk of damaging the valve seatings. Scrape off every trace of carbon and burnish the underside of the head with a wire brush.

2 Thoroughly clean the cylinder-block and manifold mating faces of the head, taking particular care not to score them.

Special Notes

An electric drill, used with a selection of rotary wire brushes, is a labour-saving asset when carrying out this work.

Removing and Cleaning the Valves

The valve spring caps are retained by split-cone collets and a valve-spring compressor is needed to remove them.

To remove the valves from push-rod engines:

1 Compress each valve spring with the spring-compressor until the spring cap is clear of the split collets. If the collets stick, tap the valve cap with a plastic-faced hammer. Remove the collets and release the spring.

2 Take off the valve spring retainer, spring and the oil seal. Draw the valve out of its guide.

3 Clean the underside of the valve heads, the stems and also the ports in the head which could not be reached when the valves were in position. Be careful not to score the faces of the valves and their seats in the combustion chambers. Wire-wool soap pads quickly remove carbon.

To remove the valves from overhead-camshaft engines:

Removal of the valves is the same as for push-rod engines, except that it is first necessary to remove the cam followers.

1 Remove the anti-rattle springs from the followers.

2 Compress each valve spring and remove the follower, placing it in the correct order on the bench so that it can be refitted in its original position.

Fig. 10. The cylinder-head bolts on 1300 and 1600 engines should be tightened in the order shown and slackened in the reverse order. A similar diagonal sequence should be used on 1600GT and 2000 engines

3 Compress the valve springs, if necessary, using the Ford locating tool to hold the valve on its seating, and remove the retaining cotters. Release the spring, take off the valve cap and spring.

4 Prise the oil seals off the valve stems and withdraw the valves.

Special Notes—all Engines

Scrape the valve stems clean. Don't use emery cloth on the sections that work in the guides. Clean out the guides themselves by drawing a paraffin-soaked rag through them.

Check each valve for fit in its own guide. If there is any noticeable degree of sideways shake, take the head to your dealer for advice. If he confirms that the valves and guides are worn, allow him to ream the guides, to re-cut the seats in the head and to fit new oversize valves. Discard the valve springs and fit a new set.

As each valve is withdrawn from its guide, place it in the correct order on the bench. *The valves must not be interchanged.* Punch holes in a strip of cardboard to take the stems and number these to correspond with the positions of the valves in the head.

Reseating the Valves

If the seating faces on the valves are badly pitted, they can be trued-up by using a valve refacing tool (your garage should be able to do this for you).

Badly-pitted valve seatings in the cylinder head can be refaced with a special tool—normally this is also a job for your garage. If the pitting is only slight, however, the valves can be ground-in in the conventional manner, as described below.

The object of grinding-in the valves (or more correctly, lapping-in) is to obtain a gastight seal between each valve and its seating. The importance of making a really good job of valve-lapping cannot be over-emphasized, since not only the cylinder compressions but the service life of the valves depend on a first-class seal between the valves and their seatings.

Valve-grinding paste usually comes in a tin which contains two grades, fine and coarse. The coarse paste should be used only in an emergency, to remove pitting when proper reconditioning cannot be carried out, but light pitting may be removed with the fine paste, grinding being continued until a good matt finish has been obtained on the valve and seat.

1 Smear a little grinding paste on the face of the valve and rotate the valve quickly and lightly on its seat with the suction-cup grinding tool, first in one direction and then in the other, by spinning the handle of the tool between the palms of the hands. From time to time, raise the valve from its seat and turn it through a quarter of a turn, before continuing the grinding. This will ensure that an even, concentric surface is obtained. A light coil spring, placed beneath the head of the valve, will make the job easier, as it will lift the valve whenever pressure on it is relaxed.

2 Check the progress of the grinding-in frequently. When correctly ground, both the valve seat in the cylinder head and the face of the valve should have an even, clean, grey matt finish with no signs of bright rings or any evidence of pitting. Bright rings are caused by grinding with insufficient grinding paste, while "tramlines" are usually the result of continuously grinding the valve on its seat without taking up a different position.

3 Check the effectiveness of the seal by making a series of pencil marks across the face of the valve with a soft lead pencil. Replace the valve and rotate it once through a quarter of a turn on its seat. Each pencil mark should be erased at the line of contact. If any of the lines are unbroken, either the valve or its seat is not truly circular and renewal or refacing of the valve or seat (or both) is required.

Reassembling the Valves—Push-rod Engines

1 When grinding-in has been completed, wash the valves and seats with petrol or paraffin, making sure that all traces of grinding paste have been removed.

2 Lubricate the valve stems with a little clean engine oil.

3 Refit the valves, and reassemble the new oil seals, springs and retainers. The valve springs may be fitted either way up.

Reassembling the Valves—Overhead-camshaft Engines

1 Refit the valves. Install new oil seals on the stems, using a short length of tube to force them into position, if necessary.

2 Compress the springs and assemble the split collets and valve caps. Release the springs.

3 Remove the Ford valve-holding tool, if this has been used, compress the valve springs and insert the cam followers, positioning each on its ball-ended stud. Fit the anti-rattle spring.

4 Make sure that the oil-spray tube beside the camshaft has not been displaced. It is important that the oil jets should strike the flanks of the cams when the engine is running, to provide adequate lubrication of the cams and rocking fingers.

Decarbonizing the Pistons

1 Rotate the crankshaft until two of the pistons are at the tops of the cylinders.

2 Stuff clean rags into the bores of the remaining cylinders and into the water-ways and other openings in the cylinder block.

3 Remove the carbon from the piston crowns with a suitable blunt scraper, taking care not to score the surfaces. Then burnish the crowns with a wire brush.

Special Notes

Do not use an abrasive, such as metal polish, on the pistons, owing to the risk of particles being trapped in the piston-ring grooves or between the rings and the cylinder walls.

Most authorities recommend that a narrow ring of carbon should be left around the edge of each piston crown and around the top edge of each cylinder bore, the theory being that these form useful oil seals if the piston rings and bores are no longer in perfect condition. There are conflicting views on this but it does no harm to play safe. This is where an old piston ring comes into the picture: placed on top of the piston, it protects the carbon seals from the scraper and the wire brush.

Replacing the Cylinder Head on Push-rod Engines

Before refitting the cylinder head, make sure that the piston crowns, cylinder walls and the top of the block are scrupulously clean. Pour a small quantity of engine oil around each bore so that it will be distributed over

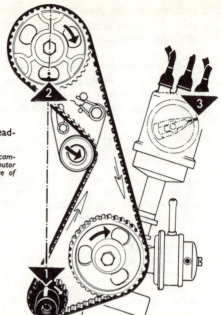

Fig. 11. Timing an overhead-camshaft engine

1, the crankshaft pulley keyway; 2, camshaft wheel timing marks; 3, distributor rotor aligned with mark on flange of distributor

the cylinder walls and down the sides of the pistons when the engine is first rotated.

Do not use gasket cement on the cylinder-head gasket, as this is likely to cause subsequent leakage, A jointing compound such as Wellseal or Hermetite should, however, be used on all other gaskets and sealing washers.

1 Refit the inlet and exhaust manifold, the carburettor and the thermo-stat housing.

2 Lay the gasket on the cylinder block, making sure that it is the right way up and that the openings register with the water-transfer holes in the cylinder block. Fit the two locating studs (*see* page 23), one at each end of the block, diagonally opposite to each other.

3 Place the cylinder head on the gasket. Remove the locating studs and fit the two remaining bolts. The cylinder-head retaining bolts should be tightened progressively, in the sequence shown in Fig. 10, to a torque of 65–70 lb ft (9–9·7 kg m). This is the equivalent to a firm pull on a spanner of normal length.

4 Place the push-rods in position, making sure that they locate in their respective tappets.

5 Slacken off the tappet-adjusting screws fully and fit the rocker shaft assembly, making sure that the adjusting screws engage properly in the push-rod cups. Tighten the rocker-bracket bolts down evenly, fingertight, and then tighten the bolts progressively to a torque of 15–18 lb ft (2·07–2·49 kg m).

6 Adjust the valve clearances as described on page 20.

Replacing the Cylinder Head on Overhead-camshaft Engines

When refitting the cylinder head it will be necessary to obtain the correct valve timing and ignition timing. Fig. 11 shows the relative positions of timing marks.

1 Turn the engine until Nos. 1 and 4 cylinders are at top-dead-centre.

2 With the cogged belt disconnected from the pulley on the auxiliary shaft, and the cap removed from the ignition distributor, turn the pulley until the distributor rotor is lined up with the timing mark in the rim of the distributor body.

3 Screw a locating stud into each end of the cylinder block, on the carburettor side of the engine, make sure that the mounting faces of the cylinder head and the block are scrupulously clean and fit the gasket to the block. The locating studs will keep it in the correct position while the head is being fitted.

4 Screw in the cylinder-head bolts, except for those in the holes temporarily occupied by the locating studs, and tighten the bolts finger-tight only. Remove the locating studs and substitute the bolts.

5 Tighten all the bolts in the order shown in Fig. 10, progressively in two stages. It is preferable to use a torque wrench, first tightening the bolts to between 29–40 lb ft (4·25–5 kg m), and finally tightening them at this stage to 40–50 lb ft (5·5–7 kg m).

6 Turn the camshaft until the pointer is aligned with the timing mark (Fig. 11). Fit the driving belt, making sure that it is engaged properly with the crankshaft pulley and the auxiliary shaft pulley, and that the latter is not rotated, as this would upset the ignition timing.

7 Slacken the locking bolt on the jockey-pulley plate, allowing the pressure of the spring to tension the belt. Turn the engine through two full turns and retighten the locking bolt. Fit the guard to the belt drive.

8 Fit a new gasket to the rocker cover, install the cover and tighten the bolts evenly and progressively, working from side to side and beginning at the rear end of the cover. If a torque wrench is used, tighten the bolts to $3\frac{1}{2}$–5 lb ft (0·5–0·7 kg m).

Special Notes

After final reassembly—see next section—the engine should be run for at least 20 minutes, when the rocker cover should be removed and the cylinder head bolts tightened down to 64½–79 lb ft (9–11 kg m).

Final Assembly

1 Adjust the valve clearances as described on page 20.

2 Complete the remainder of the reassembly, which is quite straight-forward.

3 After a final check all round, refill the cooling system and start the engine.

4 If a heater is fitted, check the level of the water in the radiator header tank after the engine has been running for a few minutes.

5 When the engine is hot, switch off and go over the cylinder-head and manifold nuts again. The bolts should be checked a second time after about 300 miles of running. With push-rod engines, remember to readjust the valve clearance on each occasion, as they will be reduced when the cylinder head is pulled down.

5 The cooling system

Maintenance of the cooling system could not be simpler, yet so often in a summer traffic jam, or on a mountain road, one sees cars stranded by the roadside with their bonnets raised while their drivers wait for their engines to cool down. What causes these "brew-ups"? A slack or broken fan belt, perhaps, or furred-up water passages, or possibly a dud thermostat or an inefficient water pump. In this chapter we shall try to explain how the practical owner can avoid this sort of trouble by efficient maintenance.

How the System Works. A pressurized water-cooling system is used on all models. The radiator filler cap incorporates a spring-loaded valve which opens when the pressure in the system reaches about 13 lb per sq in. (0·91 kg per sq cm), maintaining the coolant at well above atmospheric pressure and thus raising the boiling point to prevent "brew-ups" on steep hills and in traffic jams.

When the engine is hot and the system is under pressure, remove the filler cap carefully (normally it is best to remove it only when the engine is cold). Otherwise the sudden relief of pressure in the system may cause violent boiling and the eruption of a geyser of water and steam from the filler. *Pressure must always be released slowly*, as explained under "Topping-up the Radiator Header Tank."

A second spring-loaded valve in the expansion tank cap works in the opposite direction to the main valve, preventing the development of a vacuum in the cooling system when the engine cools down. If this valve were not provided, the hoses would collapse and the radiator might be damaged.

The water is circulated by a pump which is mounted at the front of the engine. Water is drawn from the base of the radiator, forced through the cylinder block and cylinder head and returned to the header tank at the top of the radiator. A current of air is blown through the radiator by a fan which is attached to the water pump spindle and which is driven by a vee-belt from the crankshaft pulley.

A thermostat is provided in the water off-take from the cylinder head to restrict the flow of coolant to the radiator until the engine reaches its normal running temperature, thus ensuring quicker warming-up and greater engine efficiency. More information about this important item will be found on pages 40–1. When an interior heater is fitted, some of the water is bled off to pass through the radiator in the heaters, before returning to the engine.

Anti-freeze solution must be used in the cooling system when there is any risk of frost. As a good anti-freeze preparation contains special inhibitors which prevent corrosion throughout the cooling system, however, there is everything to be said for using anti-freeze throughout the year. Further notes on this subject will be found on pages 38–9.

Cooling System Troubles. Apart from leakage, the troubles which are most likely to be encountered are overcooling or overheating of the engine. Overcooling is almost invariably caused by a faulty thermostat. It is a more serious fault than is generally realized and should be put right as quickly as possible, since it results in unnecessarily high fuel consumption and the risk of corrosion of the cylinder bores—apart from the discomfort of an inefficient heater during the winter months.

Overheating, however, is probably the most common complaint as far as the cooling system is concerned. It will occur if deposits of lime or rust are allowed to build up in the water passages, but can also be caused by other faults—*see* Chapter 12. Here we shall be dealing only with cooling system faults.

Flushing the system, as described on pages 41–2, will often cure the trouble, but remember that an unrestricted flow of air through the radiator is as important as a free flow of water. The small air passages often become clogged with an accumulation of dust and insects.

It may be possible for a garage to clean the passages by using a compressed-air gun *from the engine side of the radiator*, so that dust, gnats and flies are blown out by the air blast.

If flushing-out the system and blowing-out the air passages is unsuccessful, it will be necessary to remove the radiator, so that the film-block can be thoroughly cleaned—or renewed, if necessary—by a radiator specialist. The trouble may be caused by deposits of hard scale in the water passages, which will not respond to flushing or even to the use of a proprietary descaling compound, as described on pages 41–2.

If the water pump is faulty, or water is leaking from the drain hole in the underside of the pump body, it is not too difficult to remove the pump and to fit a replacement. Don't try to overhaul the pump yourself. Service tools are needed to dismantle and reassemble it.

Remember that overheating can be caused by faults other than those in the cooling system—see the chart on page 109.

Improving the Efficiency of the System. Although an engine-driven fan is needed to force air through the radiator when the engine is idling, or when driving slowly in traffic or climbing long hills, under most driving conditions the fan does little useful work, although it is absorbing engine

Fig. 12. The radiator and filler cap. The thermostat housing is shown
at 1. Make sure that the sealing washer, 2, is in good condition

power. The natural airflow through the radiator gives adequate cooling
at normal road speeds.

It is for this reason that accessory firms have developed electrically-
driven fans, controlled by a thermostatic switch inserted in the top
radiator hose or in the radiator header tank, which brings the fan into
action only when the water temperature reaches a safe upper limit, and
switches it off when the normal running temperature has been restored.

Details of an electric fan can be obtained from Kenlowe Accessories
and Co., Ltd., Burchetts Green, Maidenhead, Berkshire.

Aerofan Ltd., Broadway, Worcestershire, make a pitch-controlled fan,
the blades of which "feather" as the engine speed rises. This is considerably
less expensive than the electrically-driven type.

ROUTINE MAINTENANCE

W-2: Topping-up the Cooling System

As already explained, the water-level should normally be checked when the
system is cold. If the engine is hot, place a cloth over the filler cap and
turn it *slowly* until the safety stop is reached. *Allow all steam or air pressure
to escape.*

1 Press the cap downwards against the spring and rotate it further until it can be lifted off.

2 Top-up the radiator header tank until the water is 1 in. (25 mm) below the base of the filler.

3 Refit the filler cap and run the engine until it reaches normal temperature. Check for leaks.

Special Notes

When a cap is replaced it must always be tighened down fully—not just to the first stop.

If frequent topping-up is needed, check the system for leaks (*see* page 39). If anti-freeze is in use (*see* below), *top-up with water/anti-freeze mixture.* Most garages have special hydrometers to check the specific gravity of the solution in the cooling system—and thus the margin of safety—and will usually offer this service free of charge.

Using Anti-freeze. It is unwise to rely on draining off the water when the car is not in use in cold weather, to prevent damage by frost. The interior heater, for example, is not drained by opening the drain plugs at the base of the radiator and in the cylinder-block. The safest plan is, therefore, to use an anti-freeze solution, which will also help to prevent corrosion of the metals in the system.

While there will be no risk of a cracked cylinder block or a damaged radiator if an anti-freeze mixture is used in the proportions recommended in the accompanying table, the solution will form ice crystals at low temperatures which will prevent an adequate flow through the water pump and may cause severe overheating. In these conditions the engine must be allowed to idle for at least five minutes after being started from cold, to allow the system to warm up.

To obtain complete protection at very low temperatures, equal volumes of anti-freeze and water are required. Except in arctic conditions, it will then be safe to drive the car away immediately after a cold start. The cooling systems of new cars are filled with a 50/50 mixture when they leave the factory, and it is best to use Ford anti-freeze in the same concentration in future, to give adequate protection against corrosion of the system.

PROTECTION GIVEN BY ANTI-FREEZE MIXTURES

Anti-freeze (per cent in water)	Crystals begin to form		Solution is frozen solid	
	°C	°F	°C	°F
25	−13	9	−26	−15
33⅓	−19	−2	−36	−33
50	−36	−33	−48	−53

A first-class, fully-inhibited anti-freeze which complies with BS 3151 or 3152 can be left in the system for 36,000 miles or two years, but it is better to drain it off each spring and to refill with new anti-freeze, since the anti-corrosion inhibitors which are incorporated in the ethylene-glycol mixture slowly lose their effectiveness.

6-5: Checking the Cooling System for Leaks

It is often difficult to trace the source of a small leak which calls for frequent topping-up of the radiator. Perished water hoses are likely culprits. Get the engine really hot and rev it up while carefully examining each hose. If the hoses seem to be sound, have the radiator pressure cap checked by a garage. It is a good plan to renew the hoses and the pressure cap every two years.

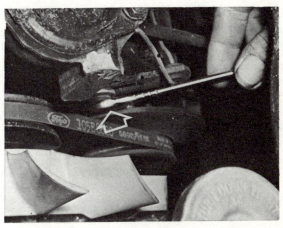

Fig. 13. Adjusting the fan-belt tension when a dynamo is fitted. The arrow indicates the clamping bolt on the strut

Sometimes internal seepage occurs past the cylinder-head gasket. Tighten the cylinder head nuts progressively, *using a torque wrench*, to a torque of 65 lb ft (9 kg m). If necessary, ask a garage to do this for you.

A preparation known as Bars Leaks, obtainable from garages and accessory shops, will usually cure internal seepages and external leaks very effectively and it is an inexpensive precaution to add it to the cooling water whenever the system is flushed-out and refilled.

6-6: Adjusting the Fan and Generator Driving Belt

The fan belt, which also drives the alternator or dynamo, should be kept correctly tensioned. It should be possible to deflect the centre of the belt between the generator and fan pulleys by about ½ in. (13 mm), using thumb pressure. If the belt is too slack, it will slip; if it is too tightly adjusted, excessive wear will occur on the fan and generator bearings.

To adjust the tension on the belt:

1 Slacken the nuts on the two mounting bolts on the generator bracket and the bolt on the adjusting strut.

2 Swing the generator outwards to increase the tension in the belt, or inwards to decrease it.

3 Tighten the pivot bolts and strut bolts firmly.

4 Re-check the tension on the belt.

Special Notes

It is not advisable to use any leverage to move the dynamo, unless the pivots and strut are binding, making it difficult to obtain sufficient tension on the belt by hand. With an alternator, *lever only on the drive-end bracket*.

The belt must be kept free from grease or oil. If it develops a squeak or a whistle, dust it with French chalk, smear the edges with a little brake fluid, or spray them lightly with silicone rubber lubricant from an Aerosol can.

Eventually the limit of the available adjustment will be reached and a new belt must be fitted. It is always advisable to carry a spare. In an emergency a nylon stocking will serve as a get-you-home substitute for the belt.

The Thermostat. As explained earlier, the thermostat, which regulates the cooling water temperature, vitally affects engine efficiency. Thermostats, of course, are not infallible and if overheating occurs, or if the engine is slow to warm-up, it is logical to check this item; but remember that overheating can be caused by a number of other faults (*see* the chart in Chapter 12).

12-6: Checking the Thermostat

1 Drain the cooling system to below the level of the cylinder-head water outlet.

2 Disconnect the water hose, remove the securing bolts and take off the water outlet. The gasket should preferably be renewed.

3 Remove the thermostat. In the case of overhead-camshaft engines, the spring-wire retainer must be prised out and the seal should also be extracted and checked.

4 If the thermostat valve is open, discard the unit and fit a replacement, which should be the wax-filled capsule type. If the valve is closed, place the thermostat in a pan of boiling water. If the valve does not open, the thermostat is faulty. If a kitchen thermometer is available, the opening temperature can be checked while moving the thermostat about in the

pan of water. Do not let it rest on the bottom of the pan. When a new
thermostat is tested, the valve should open at the temperature given in
Chapter 1. A used thermostat will give slightly less precise control of
the cooling water temperature.

5 When refitting the thermostat, clean the joint faces of the housing and
use a new gasket if there is any doubt concerning the original. The
word "Top" stamped on the flange of the thermostat must be uppermost.

Special Notes

Before refitting a used thermostat, make sure that the small air-release
hole in the valve is not choked; otherwise an air-lock is likely to occur
when the cooling system is refilled.

Many authorities recommend that the thermostat should be changed
every two years, as corrosion, deposits of sludge or hard scale, or a
distorted valve, can all cause sluggish action.

12-6: Flushing and Descaling the Cooling System

Once a year, or every 12,000 miles, the system should be drained, flushed-
out and refilled:

1 Remove the radiator filler cap (*see* the caution on pages 35 and 37).
Open the drain plug in the underside of the radiator bottom tank and
the plug or tap in the side of the engine cylinder block. If a heater is
fitted, set the controls to "Hot."
2 Insert a hose in the filler neck and allow a gentle flow of water to pass
through the system until clean water issues from the plug holes.
3 Refit the drain plugs, refill the system slowly to prevent air-locks, and
if a heater is fitted, open the heater valve, slacken the heater water-
return hose and run the engine until water flows from this hose.
Tighten the hose clip while water is flowing, to prevent an air-lock in
the heater.
4 Refit the radiator filler cap, run the engine for about half-a-minute,
and top-up the system.

Special Notes

If water does not flow freely from the drains, probe them with wire to
dislodge any sediment.

Before flushing the system it is an advantage to run the car for a day
or two with a proprietary de-scaling compound added to the cooling water,
to dissolve deposits of rust or scale. Apart from causing overheating, these
deposits may be sealing minor leaks and if anti-freeze is used there is a
risk that its very "searching" action may find such weak spots.

If straightforward flushing does not cure a persistent case of overheating,
ask a garage to remove the thermostat and reverse-flush the cylinder block

and radiator separately, using a special gun fed with water and air under pressure. If this is not successful, more drastic action will be required—see the notes on overheating given earlier.

If the cooling system is to be left empty for more than a short time, the cylinder block *must* be drained. If the system is only partly drained, the water pump impeller seal face will become corroded and this will cause early failure of the water pump seal and bearing when the car is put back on the road.

6 The ignition system

Many otherwise competent do-it-yourself owners are apt to fight shy of the "electrics," so a simple description of the ignition system and the various components that will need attention from time to time will probably be welcomed by the non-technical average owner, especially as it will become evident that no specialized electrical knowledge is necesssary for routine or simple fault-tracing. Those who are interested, however, will find more detailed explanations of the functions of the individual items in the system in other sections of this chapter.

Briefly, when the ignition is switched on, current flows from the battery through a low-voltage winding in the *ignition coil.* After leaving the coil, the current passes through a pair of *contacts* in the *contact-breaker*, inside the *distributor*, to the metal of the engine, before returning to the battery through the metal of the car and the negative battery lead.

When the starter motor turns the engine, the contact-breaker contacts —termed *"points"*—are opened and closed by a *cam* on a shaft in the distributor, which is driven by the engine. Whenever the points open, the flow of current in the low-voltage winding in the ignition coil is interrupted, causing a surge of high-voltage current in a *high-tension winding* in the coil. This surge (usually about 7,000–30,000 volts) is carried by a *high-tension cable* from the insulated cap of the coil to the central terminal in the moulded plastic *distributor cap*, from which is passes through a spring-loaded carbon contact to a *rotor* mounted on the top of the distributor spindle.

As the rotor turns, its tip passes close to terminals inside the distributor cap, which are connected to the *sparking-plug leads.* At the moment that the contact-breaker points open, the rotor will be pointing to a terminal in the cap and the correct plug will receive the surge of current. A spark then jumps across the *sparking-plug electrodes*, which project into the combustion chamber, firing the compressed mixture of petrol and air in the cylinder.

THE SPARKING PLUGS

The "tune" of an engine depends to a great extent on the sparking plugs. Only sound plugs, properly cleaned and correctly gapped, will give maximum performance and good fuel consumption. To keep old plugs in use until they are nearly worn-out is an expensive form of economy. They should be discarded after about 10,000–12,000 miles (16,000–20,000 km), although they may appear still to be serviceable. A new set costs less than half a tankful of petrol!

The correct type of plug is given in Chapter 1. Plugs which have similar characteristics are also available from other sparking-plug manufacturers, *but it is essential to make sure that the correct "heat" grade is used.*

6-10: Cleaning and Adjusting the Sparking Plugs

The use of a garage plug-cleaner is the only really effective method of removing carbon and deposits from the internal surfaces and insulator. A fine abrasive, carried by a high-pressure air blast, thoroughly scours the interior of the plug, which can then be tested for sparking while under pressure—a much more stringent test than sparking across an air-gap.

To check the sparking-plug gaps and re-set them if necessary:

1 Pull off the connectors and unscrew the plugs. Keep the spanner square to avoid cracking the external insulators.

2 Clean the points with a wire brush. If the internal insulators are dirty, or the plugs have been in service for more than 5,000 miles (8,000 km) have them cleaned by a garage.

3 Set the gap between the points to 0·025 in. (25 thousandths of an inch, 0·63 mm), using an inexpensive gauge and setting tool such as the Champion gap-servicing tool sold by accessory shops, and bending the *side* electrode only. If you must use pliers or a screwdriver, don't exert leverage against the central electrode. This may crack the internal insulator and the plug must then be scrapped.

4 Clean the threaded portion of each plug with a stiff brush and smear a trace of graphite grease on the threads.

5 Blow or wipe any dust or grit out of the plug recesses in the cylinder head. Make sure that the sealing washers are in place and screw the plugs home by turning the plug spanner *without using the tommy-bar*. Use the bar only for the final half-turn to ensure a gastight joint.

Special Notes

Over-tightening is unnecessary and is likely to lead to trouble. If the plugs cannot be screwed in easily by hand, ask your local garage to clean-up the threads in the cylinder head with a plug-thread tap, or make a tap by filing three or four v-shaped notches across the threads of an old plug, spaced around the plug so as to produce a series of cutting surfaces.

THE IGNITION COIL

The sparking plugs receive their current from the ignition coil, which converts the 12-13 volts from the battery and charging system into the very high voltage that is needed to produce a spark at the plug points.

Special Starting Circuit. An interesting feature that the Cortina engines share with some other modern power units is the provision for ensuring a good spark when starting from cold. Owing to the heavy current taken by the starter motor, the voltage available at the ignition coil may fall to only 9–10 volts, instead of the nominal 12 volts, and this will obviously reduce the efficiency of the ignition coil.

To overcome this difficulty, a low-voltage ignition coil is used, capable of providing a strong spark when supplied with the reduced battery voltage. When the starter switch is operated, the coil receives current through a wire which is connected to a third terminal on the solenoid switch which operates the starter motor—not from the ignition switch itself.

When the engine is running and the dynamo is producing 12–13 volts, however, and the coil is receiving current in the normal way through the ignition switch, the voltage at the coil would be too high. To prevent this, a special resistance wire (coloured white, with a pink tracer and having a resistance of 1·4–1·6 ohms) connects the coil to the ignition switch and reduces the voltage to the correct figure.

The effectiveness of the special cold-starting circuit depends on sound connections at each end of the wire connecting the ignition coil to the solenoid starter switch. Check these first if starting troubles are experienced in cold or damp weather.

The cost of a thorough check of the ignition system at 6,000-mile intervals, using modern electronic test-tune equipment which is available at many garages, is always well worthwhile.

Special Notes

The coil requires little or no attention, apart from keeping the external surface clean—particularly the moulded cap. A current which reaches a normal peak of about 12,000 volts (or more, if the plug gaps are too wide) will always try to find a leakage path from the central terminal to one of the low-tension terminals or to the earthed metal case of the coil. Moisture or greasy dirt is very liable to form such a conducting path.

A coil may be satisfactory when cold, or for a short period after the engine has been started, but may develop a partial or complete breakdown in the windings when it has become thoroughly warmed-up, causing misfiring or ignition failure. As it will resume its normal action as soon as it cools down, this can often prove a very difficult fault to diagnose, but it will show up on an electronic test set. Otherwise, the only practicable test is to substitute, temporarily, a coil that is known to be in good condition.

THE IGNITION DISTRIBUTOR

As already explained, the distributor directs the high-tension current from the ignition coil to the sparking plugs in the correct firing sequence. It also contains a contact-breaker, which interrupts the low-voltage current passing from the battery through the ignition coil, and automatic-timing devices (described in more detail later) that vary the timing of the sparks at the plugs to suit the engine running-conditions at any moment.

Fig. 14. Servicing points on an Autolite ignition distributor. The Bosch distributor is very similar

1, *vacuum-advance pipe connection;* 2, *grommet for low-tension lead;* 3, *cam;* 4, *capacitor;* 5, *opening through which advance-retard mechanism can be lubricated;* 6, *contact points;* 7, *one of two screws securing contact plate;* 8, *capacitor lead connection;* 9, *low-tension lead connection;* 10, *vacuum timing control*

An Autolite distributor (Fig. 16) is fitted to 1300, 1600 and 1600GT engines and either an Autolite or a Bosch unit (Fig. 17) to the 2000 overhead-camshaft engines.

The practical aspects of distributor servicing are quite straightforward, and the various parts can be easily identified in the illustrations.

6-11: Lubricating the Ignition Distributor

1 Remove the moulded cap from the distributor and pull or gently prise the rotor off the end of the central shaft. Apply two drops of engine oil to the lubricating pad at the top of the shaft.

2 Smear the faces of the cam with a trace of grease.

3 Squirt a few drops of engine oil through the hole in the contact-breaker baseplate through which the distributor spindle passes.

4 Replace the rotor, making sure that the driving lug on its underside engages correctly with the slot in the spindle. Push it home as far as possible.

Special Notes

Over-lubrication should be avoided. If grease or oil is thrown on to the contact points, it will become carbonized and cause misfiring.

6-11: (contd.) Inspecting and Renewing the Distributor Contact Points

If the distributor has not been removed from the engine a mirror, and possibly an inspection lamp, will be useful when examining the points; but it is assumed that they will in any case be removed from the distributor itself, for closer examination and truing-up or renewal.

1 Pull off the rotor. If it is a tight fit, gentle leverage can be applied with the tip of a screwdriver, taking care not to crack the plastic.

2 Lever the pivoted contact away from the fixed one. The contact surfaces should have a clean, frosted appearance, apart from the development of a small "pip" and crater.

3 If the contacts are dirty or pitted, remove them and fit a replacement set. If replacements are not available, true-up the existing points with a carborundum stone to remove as much of the pitting as possible, keeping the faces square to each other. The method of dismantling the assemblies is clearly shown in Figs. 16 and 17.

Special Notes

Always fit a new set of contacts—unless for some reason a replacement set is unobtainable. Wipe the protective coating off the points with petrol before installing them and lightly smear the cam faces with the grease supplied.

6-11 (contd.): Adjusting the Contact-breaker Gap

When the new contact-breaker points have been fitted or the old points have been cleaned-up and refitted, the gap should be adjusted.

1 Turn the engine until the fibre block is exactly on the crest of one of the "humps" of the cam. A slight movement of the cam in either direction will give a false reading.

2 Slacken the screw or screws that retain the fixed contact plate and move the plate to give the gap quoted on page 1.

3 Tighten the securing screw(s) and recheck the gap. This may be altered when the screws are tightened.

Special Notes

The gap between the contact-breaker points should never be measured with a feeler gauge unless the points have previously been trued-up. After only a few hundred miles of running, a small "pip" forms on one point and a

Fig. 15. Adjusting the contact-breaker gap of an Autolite distributor. The Bosch pattern is similar. After slackening the two screws securing the contact plate (one of which is shown at 1), the plate is moved to give the correct gap between the points, measured with the feeler gauge, 2

corresponding "crater" on the other, owing to the transference of microscopic particles of metal by the spark that occurs whenever the points open. The "pip" renders it impossible to obtain a correct reading with a feeler gauge.

Badly-burnt or pitted points should always be renewed. It is difficult to keep the surfaces square when truing them up with a carborundum stone.

A Remax contact-setting gauge (obtainable from most accessory shops) makes contact-breaker adjustment much easier, since there is no need to turn the engine in order to position the cam accurately before checking the gap.

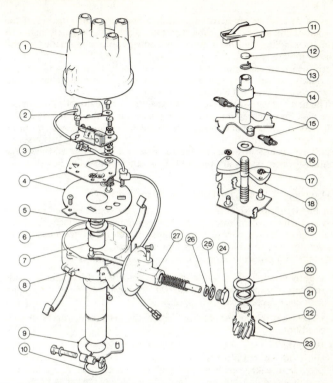

Fig. 16. An Autolite distributor dismantled. The Bosch pattern is shown in Fig. 17

1, *cap*; 2, *condenser*; 3, *points assembly*; 4, *baseplate*; 5, 6, *thrust washers*; 7, *bush*; 8, *clamp plate*; 9, *body*; 10, *seal*; 11, *rotor*; 12, *felt wick*; 13, *circlip*; 14, *cam*; 15, *advance springs*; 16, *washers*; 17, *circlip*; 18, *advance weight*; 19, *shaft*; 20, *spacer*; 20, *washer*; 22, *pin*; 23, *gear*; 24, *nut*; 25, *washer*; 26, *plate*; 27, *vacuum unit*

The Ignition Condenser or Capacitor. If the contact-breaker points are badly burned, the trouble may be due to too small a gap (which will seriously reduce the life of the points), but in most cases it is logical to suspect the condenser, or the capacitor, as it is more correctly termed.

This is connected across the contact points to absorb the surge of current, from 100–300 volts, that builds up in the primary winding of the ignition coil (in addition to the current induced in the high-tension winding which provides the spark at the sparking plug) and which would otherwise cause a destructive arc across the contact-breaker points, instead of the normal slight spark. The capacitor also discharges back through the primary windings, causing a more rapid collapse of the magnetic flux and a more intense spark at the sparking plug.

An inefficient capacitor, therefore, will not only cause rapid burning of the points, but will also result in a weak spark or—if it should short-circuit internally—failure of the plugs to fire at all.

The best test is to substitute a new capacitor for the doubtful. But make sure also that there is no break or short-circuit in the flexible lead that connects it to the contact-breaker terminal post. This cause of misfiring or complete cutting-out of the ignition is often overlooked. It is a sound insurance against possible trouble to fit a new capacitor whenever the contact-breaker points are renewed. It is not an expensive item.

6-11 (contd.): Cleaning the Distributor Rotor and Cap

The high-tension current from the coil enters the centre of the distributor cap and passes to the rotor through a spring-loaded contact. From the brass tip of the rotor the current jumps to each of the terminals in the distributor cap to which the sparking-plug leads are connected, in the sequence that gives the correct firing order—*see* Chapter 1.

1 Lightly scrape the contact strip on the rotor and the terminals inside the cap to expose bright metal. *Do not file them or rub them down with emery paper.*

2 Check that the carbon contact inside the distributor cap is in good condition.

3 Wipe the interior of the cap with a cloth moistened with methylated spirits (denatured alcohol) to remove dust or oily deposits, which will provide a leakage path for the high-tension current. A cracked cap or condensed moisture on the inside or outside of the cap is a common cause of difficult starting and misfiring.

4 Examine the rotor for signs of "tracking" (*see Special Notes*). If the tip of the terminal is badly burnt, fit a new rotor.

Special Notes

If current has been leaking between the terminals it will have left evidence in the form of dark tracks on the surface of the plastic. Sometimes these can be removed by a thorough cleaning with metal polish, but bad "tracking" usually calls for renewal of the cap or rotor.

6-11 (contd.): Testing the Distributor Cap and Rotor

There is a simple way to check the cap for tracking, without using special test equipment:

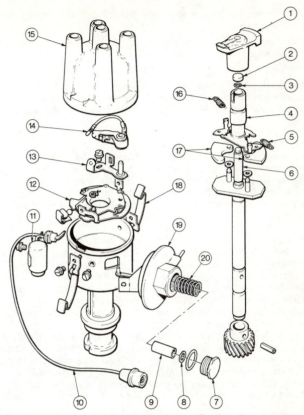

Fig. 17. Components of a Bosch distributor. An Autolite distributor is shown in Fig. 16

1, rotor; 2, felt; 3, circlip; 4, cam; 5, advance spring; 6, shaft; 7, plug; 8, plate; 9, spacer; 10, LT lead; 11, condenser; 12, baseplate; 13, 14, points assembly; 15, cap; 16, spring; 17, advance weights; 18, clip; 19, vacuum unit; 20, spring

1 Detach two alternate sparking-plug leads, and the distributor-end of the coil high-tension lead, from the cap. Insert the end of the coil lead into each of the empty sockets in turn. Leave the remaining leads in place and connected to sparking plugs.

2 Switch on the ignition, make sure that the contact-breaker points are closed, and with the tip of a screwdriver flick the points apart. If there has been any tracking, a spark will jump across the interior of the distributor cap.

The rotor can be checked for breakdown of the insulation as follows, without removing it from the cam spindle:

1 Remove the coil high-tension lead from the distributor cap.

2 Hold it almost in contact with the edge of the rotor blade and flick the contact-breaker points open. If the rotor is faulty a spark will jump the air gap between the high-tension lead and the rotor blade.

Special Notes

Occasionally, internal leakage develops from the underside of the brass electrode of the rotor, through the plastic to the interior surface, allowing the high-tension current to jump to the cam spindle and so to earth. This can be a very elusive fault to spot but will be revealed by the above test. Fit a new rotor whenever you fit new sparking plugs and you should have no trouble.

The High-tension Leads. On the high-tension side of the ignition system, we are dealing with very high voltage (7,000–30,000 volts or more) which will "flash over" or take the line of least resistance whenever possible. The high-tension leads between the coil and the distributor and between the distributor cap and the sparking plugs must, therefore, be renewed when a test, made by doubling the cable between the fingers and examining the surfaces for tiny cracks, indicates that they have deteriorated. Don't wait until misfiring sets in.

Don't be tempted to use ordinary rubber-covered high-tension cable. Make sure that you get the modern type containing carbon-impregnated nylon or cotton cords which form high-resistance conductors, to suppress ignition interference with radio and television sets. These cables (which are obtainable from your dealer) must *not* be cut and no attempt should be made to fit new terminals to them—the result will be a poor contact which will spark inside the insulation and burn the conductor away. *Complete sets of cables must be fitted as supplied*. Misfiring or difficult starting can often be traced to a faulty ignition cable.

IGNITION TIMING

The timing of the spark varies under running conditions. It must occur earlier as the engine speed increases but must be retarded, to prevent detonation or "pinking," when the engine is under load. Two automatic controls are therefore provided. Both are of vital importance to ensure maximum performance and satisfactory fuel consumption.

The first, a centrifugal control which responds to engine speed, is in the form of two small weights below the contact-breaker baseplate in the distributor. Provided that it receives regular lubrication, the centrifugal timing control seldom gives trouble. If a spring should break, it is essential to renew both springs. *Make sure that they are of the correct part number for the engine.* Their strength determines the shape of the advance curve, giving the correct amount of advance for any speed.

6-11 (contd.): Checking the Centrifugal Timing Control

It is advisable to check the centrifugal control when the contact-breaker components have been dismantled for routine servicing as described earlier.

The method of dismantling the distributor is clearly shown in Figs. 16 and 17. It is necessary only to strip-down as far as removing the contact-breaker assembly and the contact-breaker baseplate. Great care must be taken not to stretch or distort the new springs when fitting them.

Vacuum Timing Control. The circular housing beside the distributor body contains a flexible diaphragm. It is connected by a pipe to a point in the carburettor, near the edge of the throttle, so that the diaphragm is influenced by the fluctuating partial vacuum in the induction system when the engine is running at all speeds above the idling setting.

At moderately high engine speeds, with the throttle partly closed—under main-road cruising conditions, for example—a relatively high vacuum exists and the control advances the timing. When the engine is pulling hard at low speeds with a wide throttle opening, the vacuum is low and the diaphragm is returned by spring pressure. The contact-breaker assembly then rotates anti-clockwise and the spark occurs later.

It will be seen that the action of the vaccum control either adds to, or opposes, the action of the centrifugal control, ensuring the most effective timing under all conditions of load and speed.

6-11 (contd.): Checking the Vacuum Timing Control

Check the following points:

1 Make sure that the suction chamber does not contain any condensed fuel.

2 Test the action of the diaphragm by sucking sharply and strongly on the end of the vacuum pipe which is connected to the carburettor. If the diaphragm appears to be faulty, a new unit must be fitted.

3 Check the rubber connections at each end of the vacuum pipe and renew them if they have split or are a loose fit on the pipe. This is very important. Even a slight air-leak will affect the action of the control.

4 Renew the pipe if it has been kinked by careless work on the engine.

6-12: Setting the Ignition Timing

The basic ignition timing can never be completely "lost" if a special point is made of checking, *before* removing the distributor, the position of the distributor body in relation to the engine, and also the direction in which the rotor is pointing when the engine is set with No. 1 piston at top-dead-centre on the compression stroke and the timing marks are correctly aligned as described below.

To set the "static" timing (that is, with the engine stationary and the timing fully retarded) is quite straightforward. On push-rod engines it is

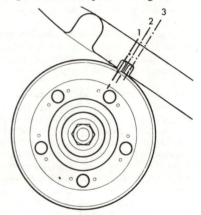

Fig. 18. One form of timing indicator. When the notch in the crankshaft pulley flange is aligned with 1, the timing is 10° b.t.d.c. Lines 2 and 3 represent 8° and 6° b.t.d.c. respectively

necessary to bring a notch in the flange of the pulley which is mounted on the end of the crankshaft, into line with the appropriate mark on the timing case. This may take the form of a numbered scale, on which top-dead-centre is marked as "T.D.C." or "O", and which also shows 4, 8 and 12 degrees before top-dead-centre. An alternative form of timing indicator is shown in Fig. 18. In this case the degrees are not marked on the timing case. On overhead-camshaft engines the degree scale is stamped on the flange of the pulley and registers with a pointer on the timing case.

So much for the timing indicator. To carry out the job if the distributor has been removed from the engine, follow operations 1–4 below. If the distributor has not been removed, only operations 1, 3 and 4 are necessary.

1 Remove the sparking plugs and the valve cover and turn the crankshaft clockwise (as viewed from the front of the engine), until both valves of No. 1 cylinder (nearest to the radiator) are closed—i.e., No. 1 piston is on the compression stroke. Align the timing mark with the pointer as described above. If you overshoot the correct position, turn the engine through another full revolution clockwise—don't turn it backwards, as the slack in the timing chain will give a misleading setting.

2 Dealing first with an Autolite distributor, slacken the clamping bolt in the clamping plate. Insert the distributor with the vacuum unit facing the front-wing valance (approximately at a right-angle to the cylinder block), and the rotor pointing to the rear of the engine. As the gears mesh, the rotor will rotate, coming to rest facing No. 2 cylinder. Fit the retaining bolt. With a Bosch distributor, the diaphragm unit must face the rear of the engine and the rotor should be at a right-angle to the cylinder block. As the gears slide into mesh the rotor should come to rest opposite the line which is stamped on the upper edge of the distributor housing. Fit the clamping plate and the retaining bolt.

3 Make sure that the centrifugal advance weights are not binding, by turning the rotor anti-clockwise and releasing it. Check that the contact-breaker baseplate is free to rotate slightly.

4 Set the timing by turning the distributor body in the direction of rotation of the rotor until the contact points are just closed and then slowly turn it in the opposite direction until they just separate. If the ignition is switched on, a small spark can be seen and heard to jump across the points as they separate.

If it is necessary to turn the distributor through a considerable angle from the initial position in which it was fitted, the gears are not meshing correctly, being one or more teeth out. Withdraw the distributor and refit it correctly as described above. When the right timing has been obtained, tighten the clamping bolt to prevent the distributor body from rotating and then re-check the timing. *Do not overtighten the bolt.*

Special Notes

A more accurate method of timing is to connect a side-lamp bulb, mounted in a suitable holder, across the two low-tension terminals on top of the ignition coil. When the points are closed the lamp will light up. At the instant that they open, it will be extinguished. When checking the opening point, keep a light finger pressure on the rotor in the opposite direction to normal rotation, to take up backlash in the drive. Tighten the clamping bolt and re-check the timing.

It must again be emphasized that the timing must not be set immediately after turning the engine backwards. The backlash in the timing chain and distributor driving gears will cause an appreciable error. Always turn the engine clockwise when making the final adjustment.

6-12 (contd.): Adjusting the Timing on the Road

As mentioned earlier, the static setting should be regarded only as the starting point for a series of road tests during which the timing can be adjusted by rotating the distributor *very slightly* to advance or retard the timing to suit the condition of the engine and the octane number (anti-knock rating) of the fuel that will normally be used.

The ignition timing is extremely critical and it is only too easy to overdo this adjustment. The usual fault is to set the ignition too far advanced. While the engine may feel very lively, it will probably be rough and the pistons and bearings will suffer. In actual fact, the overall performance and fuel consumption will not be as good as when the ignition is correctly timed.

The best ignition setting is that which gives the shortest time to accelerate over the speed range of, say, 30–60 m.p.h in top gear. It will also give the most economical fuel consumption.

7 The carburettor and petrol pump

Petrol is drawn from the tank at the rear of the car by a mechanical pump, driven by the engine, and is fed to the carburettor through a filter which is incorporated in the pump. A second filter is inserted in the pipe between the pump and the carburettor. In the Weber carburettors fitted to the 1600GT and the 2000, there is a third filter, at the carburettor inlet union.

The Ford carburettors fitted to the 1,300 c.c. and the normal 1,600 c.c. engines (but not the 1600GT) are basically the same. The 1,300 c.c. engine has a smaller-diameter carburettor throttle barrel and venturi.

When the car has a four-speed synchromesh gearbox, the carburettor has a semi-automatic strangler-type choke, but when an automatic transmission is fitted, the choke is of the fully-automatic type. Inside a housing which incorporates a water jacket, a thermostat spring and a vacuum piston both control the choke flap and provide the necessary amount of enrichment to suit the atmospheric temperature and the running temperature of the engine.

The Weber carburettors fitted to the 1600GT and 2000 engines differ from the Ford type in having two throttle barrels, each with its own jet system, housed in a common casting and fed from a single float chamber.

They are "progressive," since the throttle in the primary barrel opens first, and the secondary barrel comes into action only when the primary throttle is well open. Both throttles reach the fully-open position simultaneously.

This arrangement gives single-carburettor flexibility and economy when the engine is running on the primary barrel at low speeds and when cruising under part-throttle conditions. For maximum acceleration and high speed, however, both throttle barrels are in use and the engine then behaves like a twin-carburettor unit, giving maximum performance.

The usual adjustments are provided on all carburettors for the idling speed and mixture strength. Other adjustments, which are normally needed only when the carburettor is being assembled, such as the float setting, fast-idle speed, choke plate pull-down and choke plate opening when an automatic choke is fitted, can all be adjusted by bending the mounting arms, operating rods or tabs, as specified in the official Ford workshop manual.

These adjustments should never be disturbed in service. The correct settings call for the use of gauge rods or drills of a specified diameter and

Fig. 19. Slow-running adjustments on the Ford carburettor. The throttle stop screw, 1, adjusts the idling speed. The volume-control screw, 2, regulates the idling mixture strength

the work is definitely a job for a Ford dealer or a carburettor specialist. This also applies to the linkage that controls the action of the two throttles in the Weber carburettor.

6-8: Adjusting the Carburettor

All engines are very sensitive to correct adjustment of the idling speed and mixture strength. If an engine will not tick-over properly, or stalls in traffic or when the throttle is suddenly closed, therefore, the most likely cause is incorrect setting of the throttle-stop and volume-control screws, shown in the illustrations.

You cannot expect to obtain good idling, of course, if there are ignition or mechanical faults, but provided that an engine is otherwise in good tune, setting the idling adjustments is a straightforward job.

First make sure, however, that the emission-control valve of the crankcase ventilation system is not sticking and that the oil-filler cap is firmly in place on the valve cover; otherwise the idling mixture strength will be upset and it will not be possible to obtain good slow-running. Servicing the valve is described on page 22.

The throttle-stop screw regulates the slow-running speed. The richness of the slow-running mixture is determined by the volume-control screw. Turning the screw clockwise weakens the mixture. Conversely, a greater volume of mixture is admitted, and the mixture correspondingly enriched, when the screw is turned anti-clockwise.

Fig. 20. The idling mixture adjustment on a Weber carburettor may be as shown by the arrow, or may enter the carburettor flange at an angle

To adjust all engines:

1 With the engine at normal running temperature, turn the throttle-stop screw so that the engine will run just fast enough to prevent stalling.

2 Screw the mixture adjusting screw in or out until the engine runs evenly. The throttle-stop screw should be readjusted if the engine is running too fast, followed by further adjustment of the mixture screw. Repeat the operation until satisfactory idling is obtained.

Special Notes

Don't try to obtain too slow a tick-over. If the carburettor is adjusted to idle very slowly when the engine is hot, stalling may be experienced when it is cold. *Check by depressing the clutch pedal, or by selecting "D" if an automatic transmission is fitted.* The idling speed should not drop excessively and the engine should not become "lumpy."

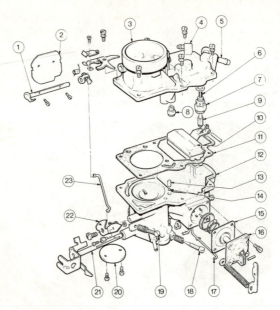

Fig. 21. Ford carburettor, manual-choke version

1, *choke plate shaft;* 2, *choke plate;* 3, *upper body;* 4, *external vent;* 5, *fuel inlet;* 6, *filter;* 7, *needle valve housing;* 8, *main jet;* 9, *needle valve;* 10, *float;* 11, *gasket;* 12, *lower body;* 13, *weight;* 14, *ball;* 15, *accelerator pump diaphragm;* 16, *accelerator pump cover;* 17, *accelerator pump rod;* 18, *volume-control screw;* 19, *throttle stop screw;* 20, *throttle plate;* 21, *throttle shaft;* 22, *fast idle cam;* 23, *choke operating link*

Next check the mixture strength. If it is too rich, the engine will run with a rhythmic beat and the exhaust may show dark smoke. If it is too weak, the engine is likely to stall or spit-back when the throttle is suddenly opened and the exhaust will sound irregular and "splashy."

The strength of the idling mixture considerably influences acceleration from low speeds. If there is a "flat spot" when the throttle is opened from the idling position, try the effect of slightly enriching the slow-running mixture; half a turn of the screw may be sufficient. It will probably be necessary to adjust the throttle-stop screw slightly to prevent "lumpy" idling, but a mixture setting that is slightly on the rich side is an advantage.

6-8: Adjusting the Accelerator Cable

This adjustment will be needed only if the accelerator cable has stretched a little or if the previous adjustment has been disturbed.

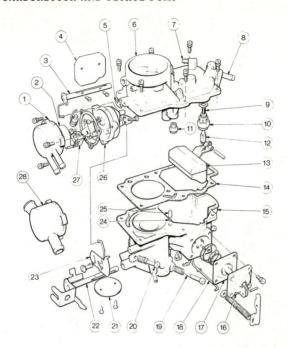

Fig. 22. Ford carburettor, automatic-choke version

1, *thermostat spring and water housing (push-rod engine)*; 2, *thermostat spring*; 3, *choke plate shaft*; 4, *choke plate*; 5, *gasket*; 6, *upper body*; 7, *external vent*; 8, *fuel inlet*; 9, *filter*; 10, *needle valve housing*; 11, *main jet*; 12, *needle valve*; 13, *float*; 14, *gasket*; 15, *lower body*; 16, *accelerator pump cover*; 17, *accelerator pump diaphragm*; 18, *accelerator pump rod*; 19, *volume-control screw*; 20, *throttle stop screw*; 21, *throttle plate shaft*; 23, *fast-idle cam*; 24, *ball*; 25, *weight*; 26, *automatic choke housing*; 27, *spring-operated lever*; 28, *thermostatic spring and water housing (o.h.c. engine)*

1 Fully unscrew the lock-nuts on the outer cable, at the bracket at the carburettor end of the cable. Unhook the throttle-return spring.

2 Hold or wedge the accelerator pedal in the fully-open position.

3 Hold the throttle lever in the fully-open position and adjust the nut nearest to the outer cable to remove all slack from the outer cable.

4 Tighten the second nut to lock the adjustment.

5 Release the accelerator pedal and refit the return spring. Check that the full throttle opening can be obtained.

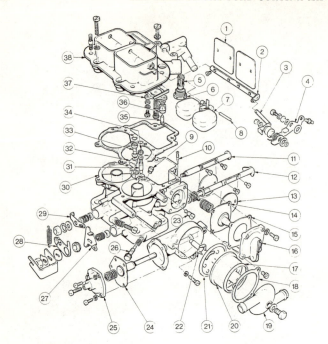

Fig. 23. Weber carburettor, automatic choke version

1, *choke plate*; 2, *choke plate shaft*; 3, *choke plate lever assembly*; 4, *fast-idle lever*; 5, *filter*; 6, *filter retaining screw*; 7, *float*; 8, *float pivot pin*; 9, *main jet (primary)*; 10, *accelerator blanking plug*; 11, *secondary throttle shaft*; 12, *primary throttle shaft*; 13, *throttle plate*; 14, *accelerator pump diaphragm*; 15, *gasket*; 16, *accelerator pump cover*; 17, *gasket*; 18, *retaining ring*; 19, *coolant housing*; 20, *thermostat spring housing*; 21, *insulating gasket*; 22, *shaft and lever assembly*; 23, *slow-running jet and holder assembly*; 24, *diaphragm and shaft assembly*; 25, *cover*; 26, *volume-control screw*; 27, *throttle stop lever*; 28, *throttle control lever*; 29, *secondary throttle lever*; 30, *lower body*; 31, *primary diffuser tube*; 32, *accelerator pump discharge jet*; 33, *accelerator pump discharge ball check valve*; 34, *primary main air correction jet*; 35, *needle valve*; 36, *needle valve housing*; 37, *spring-loaded diaphragm assembly*; 38, *upper body*

12-1: Cleaning the Float Chamber and Jets

It should not be necessary to carry out a routine check of the carburettor, including cleaning the float chamber, jets and jet passages, at very frequent intervals, but it is worth doing this during the 12,000-mile service in order to forestall possible trouble. A certain amount of extremely fine sediment finds its way past the filters and this, together with globules of water, will accumulate in the float-chamber bowl. These will cause misfiring, poor idling or difficult starting, depending on which jets become clogged.

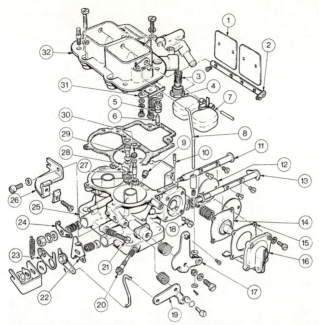

Fig. 24. Weber carburettor, manual choke version

1, choke plate; 2, choke plate shaft; 3, filter; 4, filter retaining screw; 5, needle valve housing; 6, needle valve; 7, float; 8, choke operating link; 9, main jet (primary); 10, accelerator blanking plug; 11, secondary throttle shaft; 12, throttle plate; 13, primary throttle shaft; 14, accelerator pump diaphragm; 15, gasket; 16, accelerator pump cover; 17, fast-idle cam; 18, slow-running jet and holder assembly; 19, choke lever; 20, volume-control screw; 21, fast-idle screw; 22, throttle stop lever; 23, throttle control lever; 24, secondary throttle lever; 25, lower body; 26, choke cable retainer plate; 27, primary diffuser tube; 28, accelerator pump discharge jet; 29, accelerator pump discharge ball check valve; 30, primary main air correction jet; 31, spring loaded diaphragm assembly; 32, upper body

For routine servicing it is not necessary to remove the carburettor from the engine but before dismantling it, thoroughly clean the outside, so that there is no risk of transferring dirt and grit into the vulnerable interior passages.

1 Remove the air cleaner.

2 Remove the upper part of the carburettor body and lift this off, taking care that the gasket comes away with the upper part and is not adhering to the lower casting. On the Ford carburettor unlatch the choke link as the upper body is lifted off and make a note that the choke bracket is retained by the rear left-hand screw.

3 Push out the float pivot and remove the float and the needle valve. Check for leakage of petrol into the float. Unscrew the needle valve body from the carburettor and swill it in petrol. Make sure that the tip of the valve is not ridged and that the valve slides freely in the body. If there is any doubt about the valve, fit a new assembly.

4 On Weber carburettors unscrew the plug from the underside of the upper body and remove the gauze filter. Swill this in petrol and make sure that the mesh is not damaged.

5 Wash out the float chamber with petrol, being careful to remove any sediment.

6 Remove the main jet from the Ford carburettor and all the jets from the Weber carburettor. These can be identified in Figs. 21–24.

7 Wash the jets in petrol, blow through them in the reverse direction to the normal petrol flow to make sure that the drillings are clear and flush-out the jet passages with petrol. *Do not probe the jets with wire—* this will damage the carefully calibrated drillings and upset engine performance.

8 Refit the upper body to the lower body. On the Ford carburettor connect the choke link to the fast-idle cam while fitting the upper body and position the manual choke cable bracket beneath the rear left-hand retaining screw. On this carburettor, tighten the retaining screws while holding the choke lever in the closed position.

9 On a Ford carburettor fitted with an automatic choke, fit the thermo-static spring and water housing. Locate the spring in the central slot of the lever and line-up the marks on the edge of the housing and the body of the choke before fitting and tightening the screws.

10 Remove the four screws that retain the accelerator pump, take off the pump cover and check the condition of the pump diaphragm. When refitting the pump cover, tighten the screws evenly.

Special Notes

Do not dismantle the carburettor further than just described. The rather complicated linkage that controls the action of the two throttles of a Weber carburettor, the accelerator pump stroke and the fast-idling speed of both types when the choke is in use, must be accurately adjusted, using gauge rods or drills of specified diameter. This is definitely a job for a Ford dealer or a carburettor specialist. If the linkage has not been tampered with, it cannot get out of adjustment of its own accord.

If the choke lever on the Ford carburettor is not held in the closed position while the screws are tightened the lever will be over-centre and the choke will not operate. *Do not force the lever back to the correct position*, but slacken the retaining screws and retighten them with the lever held in the closed position.

Another important point when dealing with Ford carburettors is that the accelerator pump discharge valve and the small weight which keeps it in position are exposed when the upper part of the carburettor has been removed. If the throttle is opened suddenly, the valve and weight may be ejected and may roll into the carburettor intake. The engine may be seriously damaged if this has not been noticed and they find their way into the inlet manifold.

Fig. 25. A pleated-paper air filter element is used on all models

THE AIR CLEANER

The air cleaner fitted to all models is of the pleated-paper type. It is important to service the cleaner after 6,000 miles, or more frequently if the car is running in very dusty conditions. In addition, the element must be renewed after 12,000 miles in service.

6–7, 12-2: Servicing the Air Cleaner

1 Remove the top cover from the air cleaner.

2 Lift out the element. Tap it to remove dust, or renew it if it is badly choked or greasy. *Do not* wash it in petrol.

3 When refitting the top cover, do not overtighten the retaining nuts.

Special Notes

If the air-cleaner element is allowed to become clogged, performance will be reduced and fuel consumption will be increased, owing to the restriction on the air entering the carburettor.

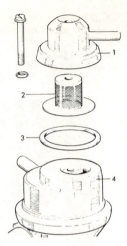

Fig. 26. A typical fuel pump. On an alternative pattern the filter is enclosed by a narrow tubular cover

1, *filter cover;* 2, *filter;* 3, *gasket;* 4, *sealed assembly of diaphragm and operating mechanism*

THE PETROL PUMP

Provided that the filter is cleaned at regular intervals as described below the mechanically-operated petrol pump should seldom give trouble. These units have a very long life between overhauls, and when a replacement is eventually needed a service exchange scheme, mentioned later, is available.

If the pump does not deliver petrol to the carburettor, make sure there is fuel in the tank (the petrol gauge may be faulty) and check that the unions in the pipe connecting the tank to the pump are tight. Also see that the pump filter is clean, that the cork gasket is in good condition, and that the clamping screw is firmly tightened. An air leak at the gasket is the most frequent cause of pump failure.

If, after extended service, the pump begins to give trouble, it is not advisable to attempt to repair it without special equipment. The most satisfactory course is to take advantage of the service-exchange scheme operated by Ford dealers, under which a reconditioned pump can be fitted at quite a modest cost.

The dealer will also be able to test the pressure developed by the pump and the rate of fuel flow, with the aid of a special test kit; and this is most important, as too low a pressure can cause fuel starvation at high speeds, and possibly serious damage to the valves and pistons, while too high a pressure is likely to result in excessive petrol consumption and carburettor flooding.

12-3: Cleaning the Petrol Filters

1 Disconnect the tank-to-pump fuel feed pipe at the union on the pump and plug the end of the pipe to prevent fuel draining from the tank.

2 Unscrew the nut on the stirrup, or the setscrew that retains the filter cover and remove the cover.

3 Pull the filter off the pump and clean the gauze with an old toothbrush or a paintbrush dipped in petrol, taking care not to damage the mesh. Brush out any sediment which has accumulated in the base of the filter chamber.

4 Renew the in-line filter, which is clipped into the petrol feed pipe. The arrow embossed on the casing shows the direction of the petrol flow through the filter.

8 The clutch, gearbox and rear axle

The drive is taken from the engine to the rear wheels by the clutch, gearbox or automatic transmission, propeller shaft and the rear axle. Attention to these items is normally confined to lubrication at the intervals specified in the maintenance schedule, when the checks described in this chapter should also be carried out.

The Clutch. Some beginners have a habit of driving with the left foot resting on the clutch pedal. This is a bad practice; even light pressure, if applied continuously, will cause unnecessary wear of the clutch-release bearing—that is, the bearing that transfers the thrust from the clutch-operating lever to the clutch-release fingers of the pressure plate—leading to noisy operation and excessive clutch-pedal travel. The same fault will occur if the clutch is slipped to avoid changing to a lower gear when the engine is overloaded. Wear on the friction linings will eventually cause persistent clutch-slip, and a clutch overhaul, which is a moderately expensive job, will then be needed.

There should be a free movement of $\frac{1}{2}$–$\frac{3}{4}$ in. at the clutch pedal, before the weight of the clutch spring is felt. This will gradually decrease as the clutch friction-lining wears, and occasional adjustment to the length of the clutch-operating cable will therefore be needed, as described below.

6-13: Adjusting the Clutch Operating Cable

1 Pull the pedal back against its stop. Slacken the lock-nut for the adjusting nut at the clutch end of the cable. Turn the adjusting nut to give a clearance of about $\frac{1}{8}$ in. (3·2 mm) between the nut and the clutch housing.

2 Tighten the lock-nut, but do not overtighten it.

Special Notes

When the clearance is correct, the clutch pedal will have a free movement of $\frac{1}{2}$–$\frac{3}{4}$ in. before the pressure of the main clutch spring is felt, as previously mentioned. For practical purposes, if this free movement exists, there is no need to measure the clearance at the adjusting nut accurately.

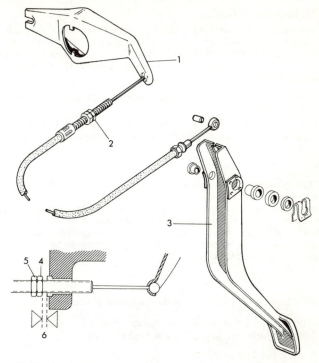

Fig. 27. Clutch adjustment is carried out at the clutch-housing end of the cable

1, *clutch withdrawal lever*; 2, *adjustment point*; 3, *clutch pedal*; 4, *adjusting nut*; 5, *lock-nut*; 6 *point at which free movement must exist—see text*

The Gearbox. A manual gearbox needs no attention, other than checking the oil-level during routine servicing and topping-up if necessary with the grade of oil specified in Chapter 1. Any oil leaks will be obvious while this is being done. If they are serious, ask your dealer for advice.

When trouble develops in the gearbox, considerable experience is needed to diagnose it with any degree of certainty. Excessive noise, or a tendency to jump out of gear, are usually caused by the cumulative effect of wear at a number of points, over a large mileage. Piecemeal replacements are seldom effective for very long; usually the most economical course is to fit a reconditioned gearbox.

6-14: Checking the Gearbox Oil Level

A combined oil-level and filler plug is provided in the side of the gearbox. To inject the oil it will be necessary to use a flexible-tube extension on the spout of an oil-can, or one of the special Castrol Handi-Pack dispensers filled with gear oil (the correct grade is given in Chapter 1). The plug can be reached from beneath the car.

1 With the car on a level surface, unscrew the plug, after cleaning the area around it.

2 If oil does not flow from the opening, inject oil until it overflows and allow times for the surplus oil to run out before replacing the filler plugs.

The Automatic Transmission. The adjustment of the selector linkage and the other controls of an automatic transmission should not be disturbed without good reason, as readjustment calls for considerable care to ensure satisfactory gear selection and the correct timing of the gear-changes. If the transmission does not seem to be operating properly, ask your dealer for advice. Otherwise, servicing is confined to checking the fluid level at the specified intervals.

6-14: Checking the Fluid Level in the Automatic Transmission

The filler-tube and dipstick for the automatic transmission are in the engine compartment, just in front of the bulkhead.

To check the fluid level:

1 With the car on a level surface *and the engine and transmission at the normal running temperature* select "P" and allow the engine to idle for two minutes.

2 With the engine still idling, withdraw the dipstick, wipe it on clean, non-fluffy cloth or paper, re-insert it and withdraw it immediately.

3 If necessary, add fluid to bring the level up to the "Full" mark. If the fluid level must be checked when the transmission is cold, it should be $\frac{3}{32}$ in. (2·4 mm) below the "Full" mark; otherwise it will be too high when the transmission has been warmed-up and the fluid has expanded.

Special Notes

Scrupulous cleanliness is essential when checking the level or topping-up. Use only special automatic transmission fluid, obtainable from your dealer. Keep the underside of the transmission free from mud—especially the ventilator grilles. Otherwise the fluid may overheat.

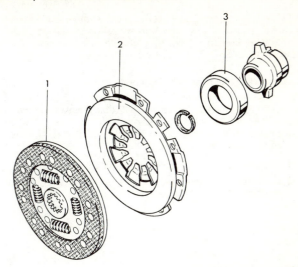

Fig. 28. Clutch components which wear in service, causing clutch slip or judder

1, *driven plate*; 2, *pressure plate and diaphragm spring assembly*; 3, *clutch release bearing*

The Propeller Shaft. The universal joints in the propeller shaft that connects the gearbox to the rear axle are fitted with needle-roller bearings which are lubricated during assembly and usually have a very long life.

Check the tightness of the flange bolts at each end of the shaft during routine servicing. Also test the joints for wear by attempting to raise and lower the shaft at each end. Loose flange bolts and worn bearings can cause pronounced transmission vibration at higher road speeds and a knock when accelerating, decelerating and starting from a standstill.

When looseness eventually develops in the bearings (usually after a very large mileage) the complete assembly of propeller shaft and joints should be renewed.

The Rear Axle. The teeth of the hypoid gears in the back axle are subject to very high stresses and require an "extreme-pressure" lubricating oil of the type specified in Chapter 1, which prevents breakdown of the oil film. The oil level should be checked and topped-up at regular intervals. There is no need to drain and refill the axle—except, of course, during an overhaul.

As with the other transmission components, rear-axle repairs are not normally within the scope of the do-it-yourself owner.

In the larger garages, assembly of the final-drive and differential gears is usually entrusted to a man who specializes in this particular type of job. Smaller concerns generally prefer to fit a reconditioned assembly which requires no further adjustment.

6-15: Checking the Rear Axle Oil Level

The combined filler and level plug is in the front, left-hand face of the axle casing. As in the case of the gearbox, a flexible extension for the oil-can or a Castrol Handi-Pack filled with gear oil will make the job of topping-up much easier. The car must be on a level surface. A special square key is needed to unscrew the level plug.

1 Wipe the area around the plug and unscrew the plug.
2 If oil does not flow out, inject a small quantity and allow the overflow to cease before refitting the plug.

9 The braking system

All models have hydraulic four-wheel braking systems, in which fluid pressure is generated in a master cylinder when the brake pedal is depressed This pressure is transmitted through pipelines to pistons in "slave" cylinders which operate the front and rear brakes. The front wheels are fitted with disc brakes, in which the pistons force steel pads faced with friction material against the sides of a steel disc which is attached to the wheel hub. The rear-brake cylinders are mounted on the stationary backplate of each brake and the pistons force brake shoes, which are lined with special friction material, into contact with the rotating drums.

A dual-line braking system, which provides separate hydraulic circuits for the front and rear brakes, is fitted. If one circuit should be put out of action for any reason, it will still be possible to stop the car. On some export models, if a circuit does fail, a warning light is illuminated on the instrument panel.

Because disc brakes call for higher operating pressures than drum brakes (owing to the relatively small area of friction pad that is pressed against the disc), a vacuum-servo, which reduces the effort required on the brake pedal, is provided as standard on the 1600GT and 2000, and as an optional extra on the other cars. The servo piston, operated by the partial vacuum which exists in the inlet manifold of the engine, acts on the hydraulic piston in the master cylinder and boosts the pressure in the brake lines by a ratio of about 2:1.

Brake Servicing. The routine maintenance required by the braking system is summarized in the maintenance schedule. From a safety aspect, the periodical checks on the fluid level, and on the condition of the brake linings or friction pads, are particularly important. The need to change the brake fluid and to renew the rubber hoses, pistons and seals in the system after 40,000 miles (64,000 km) or three years, must not be forgotten. These are also essential safety precautions.

The front and rear brakes are self-adjusting and should remain effective during the life of the friction pads and linings, provided that the checks described in this chapter are made at the specified intervals.

W-6, 6-16: Checking the Level in the Brake Fluid Reservoir

The brake fluid level should be checked at regular intervals. A weekly check takes little time and is a wise precaution.

1 Wipe the cap of the brake fluid reservoir (mounted on the engine bulkhead or on the brake servo) and unscrew it. Do not place the cap on the bodywork, as the fluid acts as a fairly efficient paint stripper.

2 Top-up the fluid level, if necessary, up to the level mark on the reservoir. The dividing baffle in the reservoir must be covered.

3 Replace the cap and check the paintwork for any drips of brake fluid.

Special Notes

Checking the fluid level is primarily a precaution, but a vital one.

Topping-up should be required only at fairly long intervals, although it is normal for the level in the brake master cylinder of cars fitted with disc brakes to fall as the friction pads wear.

If the level of the fluid in the reservoir has dropped appreciably, check the pipelines and operating cylinders for any signs of leakage. If slight leakage has occurred—say, from a slack union—air may have entered the system, giving the pedal a characteristically "spongy" feel. The method of eliminating the air from the system is described under "Bleeding the Brakes."

Check that the air-vent hole in the filler cap of the reservoir is clear. If this is choked there is a risk of the brakes dragging.

Finally, never store brake fluid in an unsealed container, or for long periods in a partly-filled tin. It quickly absorbs moisture from the air and this can be dangerous if the heat generated by the brakes causes steam bubbles to form in the wheel cylinders. It is better to buy small quantities of fluid at reasonably frequent intervals.

6-16: Brakes—Preventive Check

1 Remove the rear brake-drums (*see* "Relining the Brakes"), blow out the dust, check the condition of the linings and adjust the brakes after the drums have been refitted.

2 Check the condition of the front-brake friction pads and discs, which can be examined when the front wheels have been removed. If the thickness of the pads has been reduced to $\frac{1}{8}$ in. or if they are unlikely to last until the next service, fit new pads (*see* "Fitting New Friction Pads to Disc Brakes"). If the discs are badly scored they should be renewed by a dealer.

If one pad in a caliper is more worn than the other, there is no objection to changing the pads around in order to equalize the wear

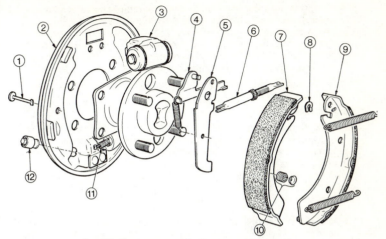

Fig. 29. Components of a drum-type rear brake

1, shoe hold-down pin; 2, backplate; 3, wheel cylinder; 4, self-adjusting lever; 5, handbrake relay lever; 6, push-rod and ratchet; 7, leading shoe; 8, "U" clip; 9, trailing shoe; 10, hold-down spring and washer; 11, handbrake cable retracting spring; 12, handbrake adjustment plunger

and to obtain a longer life from the pair, but they will take a few hundred miles to bed-in.

3 Check the brake pipes and hoses for any signs of leakage or damage, and—most important—for signs of rusting on the steel pipes, which can start within two years, and which could result in complete brake failure. The handbrake compensator and cable guides should be lubricated at this mileage.

6-16: Handbrake Adjustment

Normally, the automatic adjustment of the rear brake shoes will eliminate any excessive free movement on the handbrake lever. In time, however, the handbrake cable will stretch and it will be necessary to take up the slack by shortening the cable. Be careful not to adjust the cable too tightly, as this will prevent the automatic adjuster working.

1 Chock the front wheels securely and jack-up and support the rear of the car.

2 Make sure that the handbrake is fully "off."

3 Check that the relay levers inside the brake assembly are in contact with the adjustment plungers. When this is the case, no perceptible movement of the plunger can be felt.

4 Using the adjusting nuts located on the right-hand cable abutment bracket, eliminate all slack from the cable assembly by adjusting to give a clearance of 0·020–0·040 in. (0·5–1·0 mm) between each lever and the adjustment plunger, measured at the plunger. The cable can be pulled from one side to the other by hand to give equal clearances, if any bias exists due to friction in the system.

5 Lock the adjusting nuts and check that the rear wheels rotate freely.

Bleeding the Brakes

If, as mentioned earlier, the level of the fluid in the reservoir is allowed to fall too low, or if a pipeline union is disconnected or slackens-off, air will enter the braking system, and to eliminate it you will have to "bleed" the brakes. This is *not* a normal routine job.

A nipple that incorporates a valve will be found on each brake backplate of drum brakes, next to the pipeline union, and on each front brake calliper. You will need the help of an assistant to do the job properly.

1 Attach a rubber or transparent plastic tube to the nipple on the left-hand front wheel in the case of a right-hand drive car, or the right-hand front wheel on a left-hand drive model. Pass the tube through a box or ring spanner that fits the hexagon on the nipple. Submerge the free end of the tube in a little brake fluid in a clean glass jar.

2 If a servo is fitted, pump the brake pedal several times to exhaust the vacuum in the servo system.

3 Open the bleed screw one complete turn. Your assistant should now depress the brake pedal with a slow, full stroke, and then allow it to return unassisted. Top-up the fluid level in the master cylinder reservoir with the fresh fluid. Repeat the pumping strokes after about 5 seconds.

4 Watch the flow of liquid into the jar and continue pumping until air bubbles cease. Tighten the bleed screw while the pedal is held down fully. *Do not overtighten the screw.*

5 Repeat this operation on the other brakes, first with the remaining front wheel and then following with the left-hand or right-hand rear wheel.

Special Notes

Bleeding the brakes as just described is a somewhat tedious business, calling for two people. The whole job can be reduced to a one-man operation taking only a few minutes, however, by fitting a set of the automatic bleeding nipples which are obtainable from Halford branches or from Patent Enterprises Ltd., 143–145 Kew Road, Richmond, Surrey.

With these nipples fitted, it is necessary only to slacken the nipple on each wheel in turn, depress the brake pedal four times, ejecting the fluid and air from the pipeline, tighten the nipple, top-up the reservoir and repeat the operation on the next wheel. The fluid which is pumped out is, of course, lost, but experts do not advise re-using old fluid. Even on the first job, these nipples more than repay their very modest cost.

Relining the Brakes

Dismantling drum brakes is quite straightforward:

1 Jack-up the car and remove the wheel.

2 Make sure that the handbrake is fully released. Then remove the drum. If the brake shoes are fouling a ridge in the drum, caused by wear, the shoes can be collapsed by completely removing the handbrake cables from the underbody brackets and then removing the plunger assembly from the backplate. A new plunger must always be fitted when reassembling the brake.

3 Remove the shoe steady-springs by turning the washers through 90° and pulling off the washers and springs.

4 Lever each shoe away from its locating slot in the fixed pivot.

5 Disconnect the pull-off springs, making a note of how they are fitted so that they can be reassembled correctly. Remove the front shoe and the self-adjusting push-rod and ratchet assembly.

6 Completely remove the handbrake cable from the underbody brackets, disconnect the cable from the relay lever and remove the combined rear shoe and self-adjusting mechanism.

7 Prise open the U-clip on the rear brake shoe and remove the relay lever assembly.

8 Thoroughly clean all the parts, including the brake backplate, with paraffin. Renew any parts which are obviously worn or badly corroded It is particularly important that the adjusting mechanism should work freely. The pivots, ratchet-wheel face and screw threads should be smeared with special grease (EM-1C-18) which can be obtained from Ford dealers.

To Reassemble the Brakes:

1 Assemble the relay lever mechanism to the rear brake shoe and secure it with a new U-clip. Pinch the ends of the clip together with pliers.

2 Carefully fit the retracting springs and the adjusting push-rod to the shoes assembly, locate the shoes on the fixed pivot and prise the front shoe into position on the carrier plate.

3 Connect the handbrake cable to the relay lever, which should not be fouling the adjustment plunger, and refit the cable to the underbody.

4 Refit the shoe steady-springs, turning the washers through 90° to lock them.

5 Wind the ratchet wheel until all slack in the push-rod adjuster has been taken up. Make sure that the adjusting arm locates on the wheel.

6 Replace the brake drum and centralize the shoes by applying the foot brake two or three times. Then operate the handbrake until the clicking sound of the ratchet ceases.

7 Check the operation of the brakes by a road test.

Special Notes

Before removing the brake shoes, have ready some means of retaining each operating piston in its cylinders—a length of wire or twine will do. Otherwise, owing to the slight residual pressure that is maintained in the braking system, the piston will tend to creep outwards, resulting in loss of fluid and entry of air into the system. Make a note of the way in which the pull-off springs are fitted in the shoes.

If oil or grease has leaked from the hub bearings, the oil seal in the hub must be renewed.

It is seldom advisable to clean oil-soaked linings with petrol or paraffin and it is also false economy to purchase cheap linings from a cut-price supplier, or to attempt to rivet new linings to the existing shoes, unless an efficient lining clamp is used. The safest plan is to fit factory-relined shoes.

If the brake drums are badly scored, have them reground or fit new drums.

It is always advisable to renew the pull-off springs when fitting replacement shoes. Weak springs can cause brake judder or squeal. Some old hands recommend that the ends of the new linings should be bevelled-off to prevent these troubles, but bevelling the leading edges of the linings is apt to cause or contribute to the faults, rather than cure them. The edges of the linings should be perfectly clean and square.

Fitting New Friction Pads to Disc Brakes

It is not necessary to remove the disc brake calliper from the car or to separate the two halves of the unit, in order to renew the disc brake pads. *No attempt should be made to dismantle the calliper, in fact, unless proper equipment and the detailed instructions issued by the manufacturers are available.*

With one type of brake friction pad material, it is necessary to coat the shims and springs with a thin film of special shim grease. Ask the advice of your Ford dealer about this when purchasing new pads.

1 Withdraw the spring clips that lock the pad-retaining pins in the calliper.

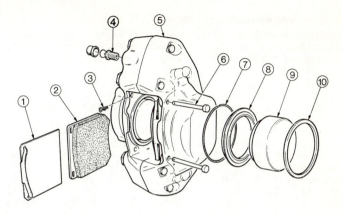

Fig. 30. A front disc brake with a brake pad and operating piston removed

1, *pad shim;* 2, *brake pad;* 3, *pad retainer clip;* 4, *bleed nipple;* 5, *calliper body;* 6, *pad retainer;*
7, *piston bellows retainer;* 8, *piston bellows;* 9, *piston;* 10, *piston seal*

2 Ease the pads and anti-squeal shims (when fitted) out of the calliper.
It may be necessary to use a pair of thin-nosed pliers to extract the
pads. Make sure that the replacement pads are of exactly the same type
as those taken out.

3 Clean the exposed end of each piston thoroughly and make sure that
the recesses in the calliper which receive the friction pads are free from
rust and grit. Sticking pistons or pads are a common cause of poor or
uneven braking.

4 Release the bleed screw and lever each piston back into the calliper,
being careful not to rotate it. To avoid any risk of the fluid which is
displaced by the movement of the pistons overflowing from the brake
master cylinder, it is as well to ask an assistant to keep a watchful eye
on the fluid level, ready, if necessary, to syphon-off any excess fluid
from the reservoir.

5 Fit the pads into their recesses, making sure that they do not bind.
If necessary, any high spots should be removed from the pads by
careful filing.

6 Replace the retaining pins in position. Preferably fit *new* split pins.
Tighten the bleed screw.

7 Pump the brake pedal several times to adjust the brakes and then
top-up the master cylinder reservoir to the correct level. It is not
necessary to bleed the brakes after fitting new pads.

40-4: Servicing the Hydraulic Components

The flexible brake hoses and the rubber pistons and seals in the hydraulic system should be renewed at 40,000 miles (65,000 km) or every three years. It should not be necessary to stress the serious consequences that may arise if a minor component in the hydraulic system should fail.

Repair kits containing complete sets of rubber parts for the various components are available, but assessment of the amount of wear or deterioration of the parts calls for experience and it is best to leave this sort of work to a dealer.

In some cases faulty braking can be traced to a choked flexible hose. A new hose—or a set of new hoses—should be fitted if there is the slightest doubt about the condition of those in service, especially if they have been chafed on the outside.

A hose should never be subjected to any twisting strain. The correct method of installing it is first to attach the appropriate end to the wheel backplate or calliper and then to fit the shake-proof washer and tighten the union nut on the steel pipeline while holding the hose union securely with a second spanner.

Vacuum Servo. When a servo is provided it is mounted in the engine compartment. It requires no attention, except to renew the air filter after about 30,000 miles (48,000 km) in service.

If the servo does not operate, first check that there is no leakage at the unions in the hose connecting it to the inlet manifold, and that the hose itself is not perished or collapsed. If all seems to be in order here, ask your dealer to vet the servo. If the trouble is more than a trivial fault and the servo has seen considerable service, it is fairly usual nowadays to fit a reconditioned unit under the service-exchange scheme operated by the manufacturers.

Should the servo fail for any reason, fluid can still flow through it to the brakes, but a considerably heavier pressure on the brake pedal will be required to obtain the same braking power.

10 The steering, suspension, wheels and tyres

Good steering, first-class roadholding and satisfactory tyre life depend on a number of interrelated factors. The steering gear, suspension, shock absorbers and tyres all enter the picture to some extent. Maintenance of the correct steering "geometry," which can be upset by a minor kerb collision, to take one example, is particularly important. The castor, camber and swivel-pin angles of the front wheels are determined during the initial assembly of the suspension, and are not adjustable. Steering geometry checks and any necessary replacements must therefore be left to your dealer. They should preferably be carried out at 6,000-mile (10,000-km) intervals (especially if the rate of wear of the front tyres seems suspiciously high), and certainly during the 12,000-mile (20,000-km) service.

The Steering Gear. A safety steering column is fitted to all models. The inner column is built up from a steel tube which fits, at the upper end, over a solid spindle to which the steering-wheel hub is attached. This assembly can telescope if the driver is flung on to it in a crash, when the nylon inserts that connect the spindle to the inner tube shear off.

The outer jacket of the column consists of a partially-convoluted tube which is separated from the inner tube by a ball-race at the upper end and by a bush at the lower end. The steering column assembly is attached to the instrument panel by a special bracket which can break away in the event of a collision. If the impact is sufficiently severe, the inner spindle telescopes into the inner tube and the convoluted outer tube concertinas at a pre-determined rate, to absorb the energy of the impact progressively.

The rack-and-pinion steering gear is mounted in rubber-insulated brackets attached to the front sub-frame. Rotation of the steering wheel is transmitted by the steering column, through a flexible coupling, to the pinion of the steering unit, which moves the rack from side to side. Each end of the rack is coupled by a track-rod to the steering arm on the wheel hub.

The ball joints which couple the inner ends of the track-rods to the steering rack are lubricated from the rack itself and are protected by corrugated rubber bellows. The outer joints are lubricated on assembly

81

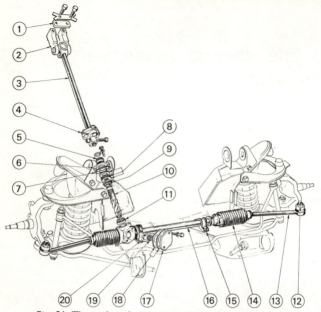

Fig. 31. The rack-and-pinion steering gear components

1, *clamp bar*; 2, *universal joint assembly*; 3, *lower steering shaft*; 4, *flexible coupling*; 5, *pinion cover grease seal*; 6, *pinion cover*; 7, *pinion cover jointing gasket*; 8, *pinion preload shims*; 9, *upper pinion bearing*; 10, *pinion*; 11, *lower pinion bearing*; 12, *track rod outer ball joint*; 13, *track rod*; 14, *rack bellows*; 15, *rack mounting bracket*; 16, *rack housing*; 17, *slipper bearing (damper) cover*; 18, *slipper bearing shims*; 19, *slipper preload spring*; 20, *slipper (damper)*

and are protected by gaiters. They do not need further lubrication during their normal life. When they develop wear, they must be renewed.

The rack bellows and the gaiters on the joints should, however, be inspected during routine servicing. Apart from allowing lubricant to escape, a damaged gaiter or bellows will also allow water and grit to enter the joint or the rack, quickly rendering it unserviceable.

A quarter of a pint (0·14 litre) of SAE 90 hypoid oil is poured into the rack housing when it is assembled and the rack should not require further lubrication unless a gaiter has been damaged or a clip has slackened off, allowing oil to escape. The steering gear should on no account be completely filled with oil, as this will result in a pressure build-up which could burst the gaiters or blow them off the ends of the rack.

Even when the gear contains the correct amount of oil, never swing the road-wheels quickly from lock to lock while the car is jacked up, as this may generate sufficient hydraulic pressure to damage or to dislodge the gaiters.

Fig. 32. The coil-spring front suspension is of a different pattern from that used on earlier Cortina models. The rack-and-pinion steering gear is also shown in this view

Two adjustments are provided to take up wear in the steering gear. To adjust the rack damper (or slipper bearing), or the pinion bearing preload, the thickness of the shim-pack beneath a cover plate must be varied. It is necessary to remove the gear from the car to do this and the work should normally be left to your dealer, as special tools must be used to measure the pinion turning torque and the tightness of the track-rod ball joints.

The alignment of the front wheels is set by adjusting the lengths of the track-rods and again this should be done only when an accurate wheel-alignment gauge is available. Makeshift methods of checking the toe-in usually lead to heavy tyre wear.

Wheel Balancing. Before leaving the subject of the steering, the import-ance of wheel and tyre balance must be emphasised. Wheel-wobble and quite severe vibration at about 60–80 m.p.h. (100–130 k.p.h.), and some-times at lower speeds, can be caused by unbalanced wheels and tyres. It is advisable to have the balance checked by a properly equipped garage every 3,000 miles (5,000 km), preferably with the aid of a dynamic balancer which allows the degree of unbalance to be checked electronically when the wheel is spun without removing it from the front hub.

The rear wheels should be balanced at the same time. They can not only cause vibration but may also cause a rear-end steering effect if they are badly out of balance.

The Front Suspension. The independent front-wheel suspension takes the form of a pair of wishbones on each side of the car, the weight being carried by coil springs, fitted between each lower wishbone and the under side of the suspension sub-frame. The wishbones pivot in rubber bushes at their inner ends. An hydraulic shock absorber is fitted inside each coil spring, and is connected by rubber-bushed joints to the frame and the lower wishbone.

The swivel axle is carried in ball joints at the outer ends of the arms. Each wheel hub runs on two adjustable taper-roller bearings. A spring-loaded neoprene seal is provided at the inner end of the hub.

Tie bars, bolted to the lower wishbone and rubber-mounted to the frame, locate the lower wishbone and provide adjustment for the castor angle. This should not be altered in service, however, unless special ride-height gauges are used to set the car to the right height before making the adjustment. The 1600, 1600GT and 2000 models are provided with anti-roll bars.

The only routine maintenance needed by the front suspension is to check the ball joints and rubber bushes for wear, make sure that the various attachment nuts and bolts are kept tight, service the wheel hub bearings and lubricate the ball joints, as described later.

The Rear Suspension. The "live" tubular rear axle is carried on a coil spring at each side of the car and is located by pairs of upper and lower radius arms, which are pivoted to the underside of the body pressing. Double-acting hydraulic shock absorbers are connected between the outer ends of the axle and the underside of the body. Again, no regular maintenance is required, except for occasional checks on the condition of the rubber bushes and the tightness of the various nuts and bolts.

ROUTINE MAINTENANCE

The Shock Absorbers. The front and rear shock absorbers do not, of course, have an unlimited life. When they become worn they will affect the steering, roadholding and the comfort of the ride. After about 30,000 miles (48,000 km) it is as well to have the shock absorbers checked by a dealer, preferably using a special test rig which enables their effectiveness to be accurately measured and recorded. Weak shock absorbers should be renewed without delay. They could cause a fatal accident.

Fig. 33. The rear suspension. The "live" rear axle is carried on coil springs and located by upper and lower radius arms. Spring damping is provided by tubular hydraulic shock absorbers

30-1: Lubricating and Adjusting the Front-wheel Hub Bearings

You may perhaps prefer to leave this job to a Ford dealer, since it is necessary to disconnect the brake hoses and remove the brake callipers. Some brake fluid will be lost and it will be necessary to bleed the brakes after the hubs have been reassembled and the callipers have been refitted.

If you do the job at home, buy a pair of new brake hose brackets from your Ford dealer. The tabs on these brackets are used to lock the calliper retaining nuts and it is unwise to bend these back against the nuts when the parts have been reassembled, owing to the risk of the tabs breaking off in service.

1 Jack-up the car and remove the wheel. Prise the dust cap out of the end of the hub.

2 Unscrew the brake hose from the calliper and drain the brake fluid out of the pipe. Alternatively, close the open end of the hose with a clean plug. A plastic golf tee is ideal for this job.

3 Bend back the locking tabs and unscrew the calliper mounting bolts. Lift the calliper away and discard the brake hose bracket.

4 Remove the split pin which locks the bearing adjusting nut retainer, unscrew the nut, take off the thrust-washer and pull off the hub, with the inner and outer bearings.

5 Wash the bearings in paraffin. Make sure that they are scrupulously clean, as even a trace of grit can cause bearing wear. If there is any

doubt regarding the condition of the bearings, renew them, or ask your Ford dealer for his opinion.

6 Pack the bearing races with lithium-base grease and half-fill the hub with grease. *Do not pack it completely* as it is essential to allow for expansion of the grease.

7 Refit the thrust washer and adjust the hub bearing. The official method is to use a torque wrench to tighten the nut to 27–28 lb ft (3·7–3·85 kg m), while rotating the hub. Fit the nut retainer and then slacken the nut and the retainer through 90° or two castellation slots.

8 Fit a new split pin and replace the dust cap.

9 Refit the calliper, using a new mounting bracket, and lock the nuts securely.

10 Reconnect the brake hose to the calliper and bleed the brakes as described in Chapter 9.

Special Notes

It is important to keep grease away from the brake disc and the friction pads. As regards bearing adjustment, if a torque wrench is not available, tighten the adjusting nut firmly and then slacken it back until just a trace of end-float can be felt in the bearing when the hub is pushed and pulled. The correct figure is 0·001–0·005 in. (0·03–0·13 mm). It will be found that the nut retainer can be placed in a number of different positions on the nut in order to line-up the spaces between the castellations with the split pin hole.

If the wheel bearings are too tightly adjusted the hub will overheat. If there is too much play, the brake pad piston will be knocked back into the calliper, giving excessive pedal travel.

30-2 : Lubricating the Front Suspension Ball Joints

Provision is made for lubricating the ball joint at the outer end of the upper suspension arm on each side of the car. Remove the screw plug, which can be seen in the centre of the slotted hole in the outer face of the arm, and using a grease gun fitted with a tapered nozzle, inject sufficient grease to fill the joint. Replace the plug.

If a suitable grease-gun or adaptor is not available, leave this job to a Ford dealer. If you have a grease gun, buy a grease nipple that has the same screw thread as that of the plug.

Lubrication of the lower joints on each side is not specified, but instances are on record in which joints of this type have failed due to corrosion and breaking-up of the ball housing. As this causes collapse of the front suspension, it is a wise precaution to remove the blanking plug from the base of each joint, substitute a grease nipple and inject sufficient grease to fill the joint.

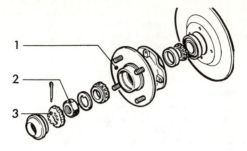

Fig. 34. A front-wheel bearing dismantled
1, *hub; 2, bearing adjusting nut; 3, adjusting nut retainer*

Special Note

It is obviously important not to continue to pump in grease when the joint is full, owing to the risk of displacing or bursting the protective rubber gaiter.

The Tyres. Apart from regular pressure checks, most authorities agree that a longer life can be obtained from a set of ordinary cross-ply tyres by changing them round at 3,000-mile (5,000-km) intervals, to equalize the wear on the individual treads. If the wheels are not changed around there is the risk, in these days of extended service periods, that damage to the inside wall of a tyre may pass unnoticed. Uneven wear caused by mis-alignment of the wheels can also escape detection.

When radial-ply tyres are fitted, however (and radials greatly improve the already good steering and roadholding), it is an advantage to inter-change the tyres from side to side at 3,000-mile (5,000-km) intervals, but they should not be exchanged from front to rear. The tyres on the front wheels develop a different form of tread wear from those at the rear. If they are changed around when the characteristic wear pattern has become established, roadholding and steering will suffer.

Radial-ply tyres should never be fitted to the front wheels only, with cross-ply tyres at the rear. *There are no exceptions to this rule and to ignore it can be dangerous.* As a temporary measure, radials can be fitted to the *rear* wheels only, but the only really satisfactory course is to change the complete set.

When rapid tread wear occurs on the front tyres, have the steering geometry and the alignment of the front wheels checked as recommended earlier. An error of $\frac{1}{2}$ in. in alignment will have the same effect as dragging a spinning tyre sideways for nearly 90 feet in every mile on the road!

Also remember that speed costs money: tyres wear twice as quickly at 65 m.p.h. as at 35 m.p.h. and fast cornering, rapid acceleration and heavy braking must all be paid for in terms of tread rubber left on the road. Another sobering thought—a 10 per cent reduction in tyre pressure below the recommended figure will result in an average loss of 13 per cent in tread mileage.

Puncture Repairs. A tubeless tyre can usually be repaired by "plugging" but this should be regarded strictly as a temporary repair. *The tyre should be removed and a proper vulcanized repair carried out as soon as possible.* Until this can be done, speeds should be kept down to about 50 m.p.h.

There is another important point which is often overlooked: when a new tubeless tyre is fitted, a new snap-in tyre valve should be fitted at the same time. The valve will last the life of a tyre, but after that there is always the risk of leakage between the base of the valve and the wheel rim.

Using a Jack. The jack engages with two points beneath the body sill on each side of the car, close to the wheel arches. Whenever possible, avoid jacking when the car is on a slope: if this is unavoidable, the handbrake should be applied really firmly and should be reinforced, if possible, by placing a chock behind one of the wheels that is not being jacked-up. If the wheel to be removed is on the side nearest the kerb, make sure there will be sufficient space to slide the wheel off its studs when the car is lifted.

And finally—never be tempted to work beneath the car when it is supported only by the jack. Always place really secure blocks beneath the axles or the frame. Better still, use properly-designed wheel ramps or axle-stands.

11 The electrical equipment

In this chapter, we shall be dealing mostly with routine maintenance of the electrical equipment, but some notes will be included on simple fault-tracing and first-aid measures.

The main components of the system are the dynamo or generator, with its associated battery-charging circuit, the battery itself, the starter motor, the lighting equipment and the electrically-operated accessories, such as the horns, direction indicators and windscreen wipers.

Strictly speaking, the ignition system should be included in the electrical equipment, but correct maintenance of the ignition system and accurate setting of the ignition timing is so important that Chapter 6 has been devoted to these subjects.

The Battery Charging Circuit. The electrical generator is driven by a belt from the engine crankshaft pulley. It charges the battery and also supplies current to operate the ignition system and the electrical accessories when the engine is running. A dynamo which has an output of 22 amp is fitted as standard to the 1300 models, and a 34-amp or 36-amp alternator to the other cars. For certain markets where a heavier current drain than normal is anticipated, an alternator may be provided on the 1300. The advantage of an alternator is that, unlike a dynamo, it provides a useful output of current even at a fast engine idling speed.

The charging rate of the generator is automatically regulated to suit the state of charge of the battery, the prevailing atmospheric temperature, and the current that is being drawn by the various circuits at any given moment.

The regulator provides a large charging current (up to the maximum output of the generator) when the battery is discharged, the rate being highest in cold weather. As the battery voltage rises, the charging rate is reduced, tapering off to a "trickle" charge that keeps a fully-charged battery in good condition.

The 12-volt battery provides the reserve of current that is needed to start the engine, and to operate the lights and any accessories that may be in use when the engine is not running, or when it is idling. At idling speeds, the dynamo does not produce any useful current, and a red warning light on the instrument panel glows whenever this occurs.

Although this lamp is usually termed the ignition warning light (because one of its functions is to remind you not to leave the ignition on when the engine is not running) it has the equally important function of warning that the dynamo is not charging. It should therefore be regarded as an *ignition and no-charge* warning light.

If the light does not go out, or glows faintly whenever the engine is speeded-up above idling speed, the battery is not receiving a charge and will quickly become discharged if the trouble is not put right without delay. First check that the fan belt is intact and correctly tensioned; then have the generator and regulator checked by an electrical specialist, or make the tests described later in this chapter.

ROUTINE MAINTENANCE

No special electrical knowledge, or expensive test instruments, are needed for normal maintenance of the electrical equipment, nor should simple fault-tracing and first-aid measures present any problems. If any serious troubles crop-up, it is best to take advantage of the service-exchange scheme operated by your dealer, under which a faulty component is replaced by a reconditioned, guaranteed unit at a fixed charge.

There is, however, another side to the picture which must not be overlooked. Although the scheme can often save time and money in the long run, some garages do tend to treat it as too easy a way out. The cost of a reconditioned starter motor, for example, is not justified when all that may be needed is cleaning of the pinion drive and, perhaps, a set of new brushes for good measure. Similarly, a dynamo may be condemned when new brushes and cleaning the commutator would restore the normal charge—work that is within the scope of a practical owner, as described on pages 93–5.

When removing and replacing the battery, or when working on the system, remember that the *negative* battery terminal is earthed. As there will be both positive-earth and negative-earth systems in use on British cars for some years to come, special care must also be taken when ordering and installing replacement equipment and accessories such as a transistor-operated car radio, which will be seriously damaged if it is connected so that its polarity is reversed.

W-4: Topping-up the Battery Cells

The liquid in the cells (the electrolyte) tends to evaporate rather quickly, especially in hot weather.

1 Check the levels at weekly intervals.

2 Don't allow the electrolyte to fall below the tops of the separators between the plates, or the perforated separator guard, as the case may be.

Fig. 35. Battery care. When a multiple-plug cover is not fitted, the individual cell filler plugs, 1, should be kept tight. Also check the tightness of the connecting bolts, 2, and clean any corrosion off the terminals, 3. The level of the electrolyte in the cells must be just above the separators, one of which is shown by the arrow

Special Notes

Distilled or "purified" water is obtainable quite cheaply from chemists. Tapwater and rainwater may contain impurities that will shorten the life of the battery. In an emergency, water from the drip-tray of a refrigerator which has been defrosted can be used, but *not* the water obtained by melting ice cubes.

Never use a naked flame when inspecting the fluid level. An explosive mixture of hydrogen and oxygen is produced when the electrolyte begins to bubble, as the battery becomes fully charged.

Add water just before the cells are to be charged, to allow the acid and water to mix thoroughly, and to avoid any risk of the water freezing, expanding and damaging the plates and battery case in cold weather.

The need for frequent topping-up usually suggests too high a generator charging rate. If one cell regularly requires more water than the others, it is probably leaking. Unless the battery is nearly new, or still under guarantee, repairs to individual cells are not usually worthwhile.

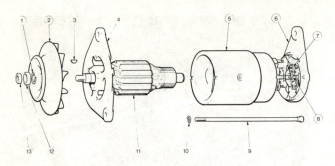

Fig. 36. Components of a dynamo

1, *spring washer*; 2, *fan*; 3, *Woodruffe key*; 4, *drive-end bracket*; 5, *yoke*; 6, *commutator-end bracket*; 7, *brush spring*; 8, *brush*; 9, *through bolt*; 10, *spring washer*; 11, *armature*; 12, *bearing*; 13, *nut*

It should not be necessary to add *acid* to the cells unless some of the electrolyte has been spilt, in which case it would be wise to have a word with your dealer.

Finally, remember that the electrolyte is a very corrosive solution of sulphuric acid in water. If any is spilled, wipe it away immediately with a clean wet cloth and then dry the part thoroughly. Household ammonia will neutralize the acid.

6-21: Battery Maintenance

The tops of the cells must be kept clean and dry, to prevent corrosion of the terminals and leakage of current.

To clean the terminals and terminal posts:

1 Take off the connectors.

2 Scrape any corrosion off the terminals.

3 Replace the connectors and tighten the retaining screws. Smear the terminals and posts with petroleum jelly to protect them against corrosion.

Special Notes

Don't overlook the connections at the earthed end of the battery earthing lead, at the starter motor and at the solenoid switch. These connections must be clean and secure.

The battery-retaining clamp should be just sufficiently tight to prevent movement of the battery on its mounting. Overtightening it may crack or distort the battery case.

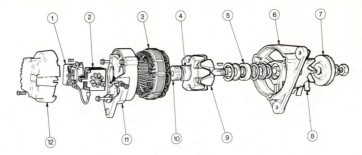

Fig. 37. An alternator dismantled, showing the major components

1, brushgear and regulator assembly; 2, rectifier pack; 3, stator; 4, 5, ball-race bearings; 6, drive end bracket; 7, pulley; 8, fan; 9, 12-pole rotor; 10, slip-spring; 11, slip-ring end bracket; 12, cover

6-22: Servicing a Dynamo

First, routine maintenance: check and if necessary adjust the tension of the driving belt as described in Chapter 5, and lubricate the rear bearing by applying a few drops of engine oil to the bearing housing.

Specialist attention (say, at 30,000-mile, 48,000-km, intervals) includes inspection and cleaning of the commutator and brushes. It is preferable to leave this to your dealer, who will also be able to check and adjust the charging regulator, but if necessary the dynamo can be serviced at home as follows.

40-1: Inspecting and Cleaning the Dynamo Commutator and Brushes

If the commutator and brushes require servicing, it is necessary to remove the dynamo and to take off the end-plate at the opposite end to the driving pulley.

1 Remove the dynamo and take out the long bolts that retain the end-plate. With the plate removed the driving-end bracket and the armature can be withdrawn. The commutator, an assembly of copper segments at the end of the rotating armature, and the brushes, can then be examined.

2 Clean the commutator. If it is scored, take it to an electrical specialist, who will skim it in a lathe.

3 Check that the brushes move freely in their holders. If they stick, clean them and their holders with a cloth moistened with petrol or carbon tetrachloride (C.T.C.).

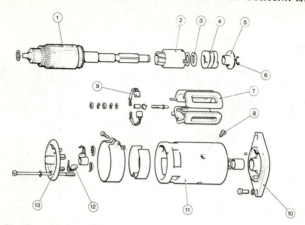

Fig. 38. The inertia-engagement starter used on 1300 and 1600 push-rod engines

1, *armature*; 2, *drive unit*; 3, *washer*; 4, *spring*; 5, *sleeve nut*; 6, *circlip*; 7, *field coils*; 8, *screw*; 9, *field coil brushes*; 10, *drive-end bracket*; 11, *yoke*; 12, *brushes*; 13, *commutator-end bracket*

Special Notes

If the brushes have worn down to a minimum length of about ¼ in., renew them. If worn but serviceable brushes are refitted, make sure that they are inserted in their original positions, to maintain the correct "bedding."

When reassembling the end-plate that carries the brushes, trap the brushes in the raised position in their holders, clear of the commutator, by side pressure from their springs, and finally position the springs correctly through the inspection holes in the plate when the latter is fully home.

Servicing an Alternator. An alternator requires no routine maintenance, except for keeping the terminals clean and the end-plate free from deposits of dust and grease. There are, however, several practical points to be remembered when dealing with an alternator which may be overlooked by an owner who has previously dealt only with dynamos.

If the battery has been removed, when refitting it first connect the negative battery terminal to the earth strap and then fit the positive terminal connector. *Never disconnect the battery when the engine is running*.

Care must be taken not to earth the "live" connector in the moulded socket if it is removed from the alternator. Never run the engine with the main output cable from the alternator disconnected.

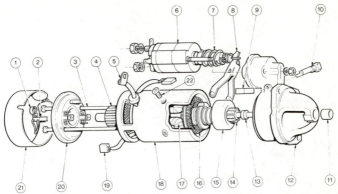

Fig. 39. The pre-engaged starter fitted to the 1600GT. The starter of the 2000 is basically similar but the commutator and brushes are differently arranged

1, *brush spring;* 2, *brush;* 3, *through bolts;* 4, *commutator;* 5, *solenoid connecting link;* 6, *solenoid;* 7, *spring;* 8, *engagement lever;* 9, *grommet;* 10, *pivot pin;* 11, *bush;* 12, *drive-end bracket;* 13, *jump ring;* 14, *gear;* 15, *drive assembly;* 16, *field coil(s);* 17, *pole shoe(s);* 18, *yoke;* 19, *brush;* 20, *commutator-end bracket;* 21, *clamp*

If a charger is to be used to charge-up a flat battery, first isolate the alternator by disconnecting both battery terminals.

An electrician who is not familiar with an alternator should be warned not to use an ohmmeter of the type that incorporates a hand-driven generator (usually known as a "megger") to check the rectifier diodes or the transistors in the circuit.

If the charging circuit gives trouble, or the alternator requires routine servicing, the work should always be done by a fully-qualified auto-electrician.

The Starter Motor. The starter motor is probably the most important of the auxiliaries that draw current from the battery. Unlike the generator, it is in action only intermittently and usually has a long, trouble-free life. Because it requires no periodic lubrication it is, in fact, often overlooked by the average owner.

40-2: Starter Motor Servicing

The starter should be serviced at reasonable intervals—say, ever 30,000 miles (48,000 km)—when it should be removed from the car and dismantled by an expert, so that the commutator, brushes and the pinion-drive components can be inspected and cleaned.

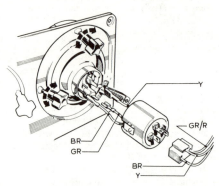

Fig. 40. The connections to an inner headlamp are shown in the upper drawing, and a combined side-lamp and headlamp in the lower sketch (for colour code, see below)

Key to wiring colour codes, Figs. 40–49

Code	Wiring colour	Code	Wiring colour
R	Red	Y	Yellow
BK	Black	LG	Light Green
BL	Blue	P	Purple
W	White	O	Orange
BR	Brown	PK	Pink
G	Green	GR	Grey

The Headlamps. The headlamps fitted to L and XL cars are of the sealed-beam type, in which the filaments are sealed in to a single glass unit which incorporates the lens and reflector. Each unit is, in effect, a very large bulb, and if a filament fails, or the lens is cracked by a stone or a minor collision, it must be replaced as a unit.

On the GT and GXL cars, and on other models for some export territories semi-sealed lamps are fitted, in which separate bulbs are carried in removable bulb holders.

It is particularly important that the headlamp beams should be correctly aligned. Hit-and-miss methods of adjustment in the home garage are likely to result in settings that dazzle oncoming traffic or do not give the most effective illumination.

Most garages today, however, have optical beam-setting equipment which enables the lamps to be precisely adjusted. The headlamp settings should be checked with the aid of such equipment twice a year if a lot of night driving is done, or at least once every autumn.

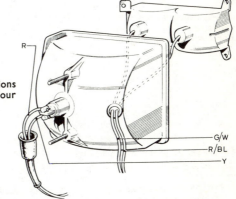

Fig. 41. Wiring connections for a rear lamp (for colour code, see page 96)

Each headlamp has two beam-adjusting knobs, which project beside the headlamp housing inside the engine compartment. One knob adjusts the beam in a vertical plane while the other moves it from side to side.

Removing and Replacing Headlamp Light Units or Bulbs

Before either type of headlamp can be removed, the radiator grille must be taken off. It is retained by nine cross-headed screws.

1 To remove a sealed-beam unit, unscrew the three inner bezel retaining screws that secure the unit to the backplate.

2 Pull the unit forward and unplug the connector, which also carries a side-lamp bulb.

3 When a semi-sealed unit is fitted, remove the unit as just described, twist the bulb holder anti-clockwise and remove it.

Side, Rear Lamp and Direction-indicator Bulbs

The method of changing these bulbs is quite straightforward. The lenses are retained by cross-headed screws, except in the case of the side-lamp bulbs when sealed-beam headlamps are fitted, when, as already described, the bulbs are carried in the lamp connectors.

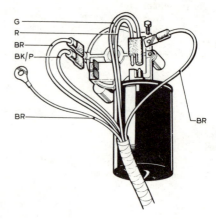

Fig. 42. Connections to the windscreen wiper motor (for colour code, see page 96)

Instrument Panel and Warning Lights

To renew these it is necessary to remove the instrument cluster—

1 Remove the choke control knob, when fitted, the steering column shroud and the facia panel.
2 Withdraw the instrument cluster.

The Windscreen Wiper. The electrically-operated wiper normally requires no attention, other than renewal of the wiper blades at least once a year.

If the blades do not sweep through satisfactory arcs, or fail to park neatly when the wiper is switched off (they are self-parking), the arms may have been incorrectly fitted to the driving spindles. They can be withdrawn by depressing the spring catch that clamps the arm to the splined section of the spindle. Refit the arm in the desired position and push it fully home.

Wet the screen before checking the sweep and the parking of the blades. A test on a dry screen will give misleading results, owing to excessive friction between the blades and the glass.

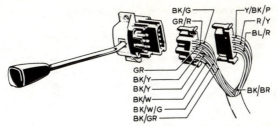

Fig. 43. The direction indicator switch, showing the wiring connections
(for colour code, see page 96)

Direction Indicators. The flashing-indicator lamps are fed with current from a sealed control unit, secured by a spring clip behind the instrument panel. If either a front or a rear indicator bulb should fail, the remaining indicators will continue to flash, but at a faster rate than normal.

Failure or erratic action of the indicators may also be caused by dirty contacts in the indicator switch, in the wiring, or by a "blown" fuse. If the fuse is in order, the flasher unit is probably faulty. It is not repairable.

The Brake-light Switch. This switch is screwed into the bulkhead in the driving compartment. It is operated by the brake pedal, the contacts in the

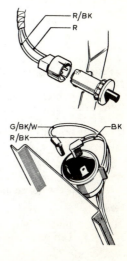

Fig. 44. A door-operated
courtesy light switch (top)
and the direction-indicator
flashing unit, below (for
colour code, see page 96)

switch closing when the pressure on the switch plunger is released as the pedal is pressed down.

If the brake lights do not light-up when the pedal is depressed, remove the instrument facia panel (*see* page 98), switch on the ignition, disconnect the leads from the switch terminals and connect them together. If the brake lights then operate, the switch is faulty, or the connections to it were dirty or corroded. If the lights still fail to operate, the fault must lie in the fuse (*see* below) or in the wiring or connections in the circuit.

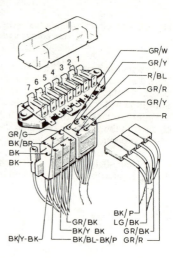

Fig. 45. The fuse box. For a key to the wiring colours, see page 96. The circuits protected by the fuses are listed in the text

Fuses. The fuses are carried in a block mounted in the engine compartment on the left-hand wing valance.

There are three unused connections, corresponding to fuses 1, 6 and 7 (*see* the fuse numbers in Fig. 45) which may be used to connect accessories. Fuses 6 and 7 are fed from the ignition switch and are "live" only when the ignition is switched on, whereas No. 1 fuse is live at all times.

All fuses are rated at 8 amps. It is important to remember this, since most of the replacement fuses sold for British cars are the 35 amp type.

The circuits protected are:

Fuse	Circuit Protected
1	Interior lamp, cigar lighter, emergency flasher
2	Left-hand side and tail lamp, number-plate light

3   Right-hand side and tail lamp, instrument illumination lamps
4   Headlamp main beams
5   Headlamp dipped beams
6   Stop lamp, reversing light, heater motor, indicator lights
7   Windscreen wiper motor

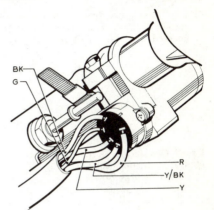

Fig. 46. Wiring connections to the ignition switch (for colour code, see page 96)

Failure of a particular fuse is indicated when the circuit protected by it becomes "dead." If a new fuse burns out immediately, find the cause and rectify the fault before fitting a new fuse having the same rating, which is shown on a coloured slip of paper inside the fuse. Always fit a fuse of the correct rating and *never be tempted to bridge the fuse-holder clips with ordinary wire*, as this can lead to a fire in the wiring, or a burnt-out component.

A thorough diagnosis of an ailing electrical system calls for the use of proper fault-tracing equipment, or at the least, an accurate moving-coil voltmeter. Ideally, a special instrument tester should be used to check the fuel and temperature gauges, so this sort of work is outside the scope of the average owner.

There are, however, some simple tests that can be made when it is suspected that the generator is not giving its full charge, or when the starter motor does not turn the engine.

6-21: Testing the Generator and Charging System

The following tests, for which only a voltmeter is required, are sufficient to show whether or not all is well with the dynamo and charging system. A moving-coil type of meter is to be preferred, but any good-quality instrument can be used, as the checks depend on comparative readings, rather than on exact voltages. They are based on the fact that the battery voltage varies according to the state of charge, and is always higher when the cells are receiving a charge from the dynamo.

To make the test:

1 Clip the voltmeter leads to the battery terminals, making sure that the surface of the metal has been pierced. If the battery is sound and well charged, a reading of 12–12·5 volts should be obtained.

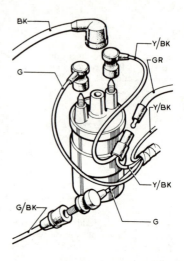

Fig. 47. Connections to the ignition coil (for colour code, see page 96)

2 Switch on all the lights. The reading should now fall to approximately 11–11·5 volts.

3 Start the engine and speed it up to the equivalent of about 20 m.p.h. in top gear, but do not race it. The reading should now be about 13·5 volts, and the voltmeter needle should be steady. If it flickers, there may be a bad contact in the wiring, the dynamo commutator may be dirty, the brushes may be worn or sticking, or the cut-out or regulator may be faulty.

Special Notes

If voltage readings roughly equal to those quoted are obtained, it can be assumed that the battery and charging system are sound. If the voltage across the battery does not rise by 1 volt when the engine is speeded-up above idling speed, there is a fault somewhere in the charging system,

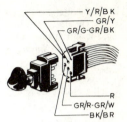

Fig. 48. The side/headlamp switch (above) and the stop lamp switch, below (for colour code, see page 96)

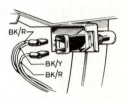

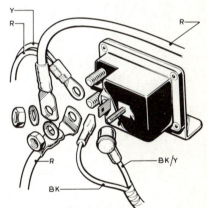

Fig. 49. Connections to the starter solenoid (for colour code, see page 96)

probably one of those just mentioned. If the increase exceeds about 1·5 volts, either the regulator is incorrectly adjusted or the battery is faulty. Do not try to adjust the regulator. Leave this sort of work to a qualified auto-electrician.

Testing a Faulty Starter Motor

1 Switch on the lights and press the starter switch. If the solenoid switch clicks and the lights go dim, but the starter does not operate, either

the battery is discharged or current is flowing through the windings of the starter but for some reason the armature is not rotating. Probably the starter pinion is jammed in mesh with the flywheel starter ring. To free it, *see Special Notes*, below.

2 If the lamps remain bright, the starter switch may be faulty, but first check for loose or corroded connections on the ignition switch or on the electro-magnetic solenoid starter switch itself.

Special Notes

To free a jammed starter pinion, switch off the ignition, engage *top gear* and rock the car *forwards*. Do not rock the car backwards and forwards, as this may jam the pinion more firmly in mesh with the flywheel ring-gear teeth.

12 When Things Go Wrong

The risk of an unexpected breakdown must obviously be greatly reduced by regular servicing. The work described in previous chapters can therefore be described as *preventive* maintenance in the best sense of the word; it aims at detecting or forestalling trouble before it becomes serious. Most faults, in fact, can be traced back to neglect at some stage. Dirt, lack of lubrication or incorrect adjustment are the most frequent culprits.

In the charts in this chapter it has been possible to deal only with the simpler checks that can be made in the garage or by the roadside. It is assumed that special test equipment will not be available, and that expert help will be called in if the trouble does not respond to first-aid measures.

The secret of diagnosing a fault quickly is to follow a systematic process of elimination. Haphazard tests seldom pay dividends—although there are, of course, occasions on which the possibility of a particular fault can be assumed with a fair amount of certainty.

Take the case of the normally well-behaved engine that refuses to fire from cold after the car has been parked in the open during a spell of damp, misty weather. Condensation on the high-tension leads, ignition coil, distributor, and sparking-plug insulators is almost a certainty, and a wipe with a dry cloth or spraying them with a water-dispelling Aerosol (such as Rocket WD–40), will usually be all that is needed to restore normal starting. WD–40 will also help to prevent condensation troubles in future.

Similarly, if an engine runs well, but is a brute to start from cold, suspect too weak a starting mixture. Make sure that the mixture control is operating properly and that the petrol pump is delivering plenty of fuel. If the engine is reluctant to start when hot, on the other hand, check for an over-rich mixture. In either case, if the carburation seems to be satisfactory, the ignition system should be carefully checked-over, following the step-by-step charts in this chapter.

Once a year, or before starting a holiday tour, there is a great deal to be said for taking the car to a garage which has electronic test-tune equipment, with which every aspect of the ignition system, carburation and mechanical efficiency can be quickly checked and any faults or maladjustments pinpointed quickly and accurately.

STARTING TROUBLES

Starter Motor Faults

Starter Motor Does Not Turn Engine	Turns Engine Slowly
Probable Fault Battery discharged or worn-out. Battery connections or earthing strap loose or corroded. Faulty starter switch. Dirty starter drive. Drive spring broken. Faulty starter motor. Engine water pump frozen.	*Probable Fault* Battery partly discharged or nearing end of life. Battery connections or earthing strap loose or corroded. Too heavy a grade of engine oil in use. Faulty starter motor.

Starter Operates but Pinion Will Not Engage with Flywheel Ring Gear	Pinion Will Not Disengage
Dirt or excessive wear on pinion drive, preventing the control nut running along the screwed sleeve. Removal of the starter, cleaning the drive and renewal of any worn parts will usually cure the trouble. Low battery voltage is also a possible cause. When a pre-engaged starter is fitted, check the solenoid-operated engagement mechanism.	If the pinion is jammed in mesh with the flywheel ring gear, a click will be heard from the starter solenoid switch when the key switch is turned. To free the pinion, see page 104.

Excessively Noisy Starter
Dirt or grit on pinion sleeve. Badly worn or damaged teeth on pinion or on flywheel ring gear. Loose starter mounting bolts or worn or damaged pinion or flywheel ring gear.

STARTING TROUBLES (contd.)

Engine Will Not Fire
Carry out the following checks in sequence (see text)

Ignition System — *Probable Fault*

Battery Check
Switch on lights and check brightness when starter is operated.
Lamps do not light, or are weak—

Battery discharged (see also pages 111–12).
Battery connections or earthing strap loose or corroded.
Faulty ignition switch.

Lights dim only slightly—

Loose connection or broken wire between switch and ignition coil or distributor.

Sparking Plug Check
Remove a plug, reconnect the lead and lay the plug on the cylinder block. Watch for sparks while the engine is rotated.
No spark at plug gap—

Condensed moisture on distributor cap or plug leads or insulators.
Oil or condensed fuel or water on plug points or internal insulator.
Sparking plug internal or external insulator dirty or cracked.
Ignition system trouble (see below).

Distributor Check
Remove sparking plug lead from plug, hold bare end of lead ⅜ in. from unpainted metal of engine. Rotate engine with ignition switched on.
No spark from sparking plug lead—

Contact-breaker points dirty, or pitted, or not opening and closing.
Cracked rotor.
Poor connections in low tension circuit.
Faulty distributor cap.
Faulty condenser or connections.
Spring contact blade on rotor bent or broken.
High-tension coil lead loose or broken.
Coil burnt out.

Spark from plug lead—

Trouble must lie in sparking plugs.

Fuel System Check
Check that petrol reaches carburettor when engine rotated by starter, by disconnecting pipe at carburettor.
No petrol reaching carburettor—

Petrol reaching carburettor—

Fuel System — *Probable Fault*

Petrol tank empty.
Choked petrol filter.
Air leak in pipeline.
Faulty petrol pump.
Air vent to tank clogged.
Blockage in pipeline.
Mixture too rich or too weak.
Water in petrol.
Jet obstructed.
Bad air leak in induction manifold or at carburettor flange.

OTHER POSSIBLE CAUSES OF DIFFICULT STARTING
Broken distributor drive.
Timing chain broken or has jumped sprocket teeth.
Exhaust tailpipe blocked.

MISCELLANEOUS ENGINE TROUBLES

PROBABLE CAUSE

SYMPTOM	Ignition System	Fuel System	Other Faults
Misfiring	Incorrect gap at sparking-plug points. Dirty or cracked sparking-plug insulators. Wrong type of sparking plugs. Damp or oily deposits on high-tension leads, sparking-plug, distributor or coil insulation. High-tension or low-tension leads loose or short-circuiting. Faulty ignition interference suppressors (if fitted) or plug leads.	Water in carburettor. Petrol pipe partly blocked. Fuel pump pressure low. Fuel pump filter choked. Carburettor needle valve faulty or dirty. Jet obstructed.	Incorrect valve clearance. Valves sticking. Valve seatings burnt. Valve spring broken. Leaking cylinder-head gasket.
Engine Fires but Will Not Continue to Run	Condensation on plug points. Low-tension connection loose. Broken wire in distributor, between capacitor and contact-breaker points. Faulty ignition-switch contact. Contact-breaker rocker arm sticking. Dirty contact-breaker points.	Carburettor needle valve sticking. Fuel pump faulty. Petrol pipe partly blocked. Jet obstructed. Water in petrol.	Exhaust tailpipe obstructed. Incorrect ignition or valve timing.
Engine Runs on Wide Throttle Opening Only		Slow-running mixture strength and or idling speed incorrect. Jet obstructed. Air leak at carburettor or inlet manifold flange.	Valves sticking. Valve seatings burnt. Valve spring broken.
Engine Does Not Give Full Power	Ignition timing retarded. Ignition timing over-advanced. Ignition faults (see under *Misfiring*).	Petrol supply troubles (see above). Throttle not opening fully. Jet obstructed.	Incorrect valve clearances. Valve seatings burnt. Partial engine seizure—(see *Overheating*). Leaking cylinder-head gasket. Low compression due to worn piston rings and cylinders.

MISCELLANEOUS ENGINE TROUBLES (contd.)

SYMPTOM	PROBABLE CAUSE		
	Ignition System	**Fuel System**	**Other Faults**
Overheating	Ignition timing incorrect—too far advanced or retarded. Wrong type of sparking plug, over-heating and causing pre-ignition.	Weak mixture (see under Mis-firing).	Filler cap not retaining pressure in cooling system. Too little water in radiator. Fan belt slipping or broken. Choked radiator (water and air passages). Lime and rust deposits in cooling system. Perished or collapsed water hoses. Faulty thermostat. Leaking cylinder-head gasket. Too little oil in engine. Tight engine after overhaul. Excessive carbon deposit or badly-seating valves— engine needs top-overhaul. Worn bearings, pistons or other mechanical faults.
Knocking or Pinking	Ignition timing too far advanced. Wrong type of sparking plugs fitted, overheating and causing pre-ignition.	Wrong grade of fuel in use— use premium grade. If this does not cure trouble, check for faults listed in other columns.	

STEERING FAULTS

Symptom	Probable Cause
Heavy Steering	Low pressures in front tyres. Inadequate lubricant in steering unit and/or joints. Incorrect steering adjustments.
Excessive Free Movement at Steering Wheel	Wear in steering linkage. The outer ball joints are self-adjusting and if slackness develops they should be renewed. Wear in steering rack-and-pinion assembly. Adjustment (by a Ford dealer) may correct this. Otherwise fit a reconditioned assembly. Steering unit mounting U-clips slack. Steering column flexible coupling bolts loose.
Steering Wander A tendency to wander and general lack of precision may be caused by slackness at any point in the steering gear (see above). Otherwise, check for faults in the next column.	Low or uneven tyre pressures. If the rear tyre pressures are too low, the car will "oversteer" and will be affected by side winds at speed. Steering geometry incorrect. Have the geometry checked by a service station which possesses first-class modern equipment. Distortion or damage to steering or suspension units. This may be caused by a minor collision and will be revealed by checks, carried out with precision equipment, against the measurements specified in the workshop manual. Normally a job for the expert.
Wheel Wobble or Steering Vibration at Speed	Unbalanced wheels and tyres will cause vibration, often at about 60–70 m.p.h. Have wheels and tyres checked both for static and dynamic balance. Incorrect steering geometry. See "Steering Wander," above. Slackness in steering gear. See "Excessive Free Movement at Steering Wheel," above. Weak shock absorbers.

BRAKING SYSTEM FAULTS

Symptom	Probable Cause
Excessive Pedal Travel	Brakes require adjustment (see Chapter 9). If fault occurs only after prolonged or excessive use of brakes, it is caused by "brake fade." Normal braking will be restored when brakes cool down.
Brake Pedal Feels Spongy or Requires Pumping to Operate Brake	Air in hydraulic system. Check level of fluid in reservoir, top-up if necessary and bleed brakes (see Chapter 9). Check for leaks throughout. Main cup in master cylinder worn. Have components renewed by service station. Excessive end-float on front-wheel hub bearings.

BRAKING SYSTEM FAULTS (contd.)

Symptom	Probable Cause
Brakes Lack Power (See also "Excessive Pedal Travel," above)	Worn friction linings or pads, or oil or grease on linings or pads. Fit replacements (see Chapter 9). Scored or distorted brake drums or discs. Fit new drums or discs. Defective piston cups or seals in cylinders or callipers. Have new parts fitted throughout. Defective brake servo (when fitted).
Brakes Bind	Handbrake adjustment too tight or cable binding. Swollen piston or seal in brake cylinder or master cylinder. Compensating port in master cylinder obstructed by grit or swollen main cup. Master cylinder should be overhauled by an expert. Defective brake servo (when fitted).
Brakes Grab	Friction linings or pads contaminated with oil or grease. Sometimes the brakes may grab slightly after the car has stood overnight in damp weather. This is not a serious fault, if symptom disappears during normal running. Loose front hub bearings. Distorted or badly scored drum or disc.
Brakes Pull to One Side	Unequal tyre pressures. Grease or oil on friction linings. Worn or glazed friction linings. Restriction in flexible brake hose or faulty operating cylinder in brake on opposite side to which steering pulls. Wear in front suspension or steering components.

GENERATOR AND CHARGING SYSTEM FAULTS

As a quick check on whether the battery is well charged and the cables and connections are in good condition, switch on the headlights and operate the starter. If the lights dim only slightly and the starter turns the engine at normal speed, it can be assumed that the battery and main wiring system are sound.

If the lights become very dim or go out when the starter is operated, check first for loose or dirty connections at the battery terminals, at the starter motor or solenoid-operated switch and at the connection between the battery earthing cable and the bodywork. A rusty or corroded contact here is often overlooked. If these checks are satisfactory, you should have the battery tested by a service station which possesses the correct equipment.

These preliminary checks should always be made before attempting to diagnose any of the faults listed on page 112.

Symptom   *Probable Cause*

**Battery Charge
Consistently Low**
A low state of charge may be due simply to the drain caused by frequent starting, short journeys and night driving, when the output from the dynamo is often insufficient to meet the current drawn from the battery. During the winter months it may be necessary to use a trickle charger regularly in such circumstances. But first check for the faults in the next column.

Defective battery. Sulphated plates will not accept a full charge. Buckled plates or an accumulation of sediment will cause internal leakage of current. Have battery checked by an expert.

Loose dynamo or alternator driving belt. Check tension of belt and adjust if necessary.

Insufficient output from generator. Have output tested by service station. New brushes may be required or a replacement generator may be needed.

Faulty generator regulator. A moving-coil voltmeter is needed when checking and adjusting the regulator. Again a job for the expert.

Loose connections or a broken wire in charging circuit.

**Battery Consistently
Overcharged**
This fault is indicated by the need for frequent topping-up of the battery with distilled water.

Regulator set to give too high a charging rate. Have setting checked by a service station.

13 Saving Money on Repairs

Major repairs are not normally within the scope of the average owner, who is often forced to work under somewhat cramped conditions. There is also the unfortunate fact that the design of modern cars calls for the use of a fairly extensive range of special tools if ambitious work is undertaken, and the expense of these will not be justified if only occasional jobs are to be done. Sometimes it is possible to do without the recommended service tool, but makeshift methods seldom pay in the long run.

It is these factors which have resulted in the widespread adoption nowadays of the reconditioned-unit exchange scheme, under which factory-rebuilt parts can be obtained in exchange for the worn or faulty units. The advantage of this arrangement, of course, is that the unit carries the manufacturer's guarantee and that repair is simply a matter of removing the old part and installing the new one.

There is, however, another side to the picture. Some garages are rather too inclined to take the easy way out and to fit a reconditioned replacement when the faulty unit could be repaired at a much lower cost. It is not surprising, therefore, that many practical owners prefer to do as much of the actual repair work as possible, thus saving not only high labour charges, but also the cost of parts which are still serviceable. An example is a partial engine overhaul, described later in this chapter.

When this has been said, one must still draw a line somewhere. For example, gearbox (or automatic transmission) and rear axle overhauls are beyond the scope of the owner, and this also applies to some other units, as explained on page 116. Experience has shown that unless these jobs are done under workshop conditions, using special tools and gauges when necessary, further trouble is almost inevitable.

Without the right tools, some jobs cannot be done at all, or at best only in a botched-up way that will never prove satisfactory. Owners are not alone, of course, in using makeshift methods. Only too often one sees garage mechanics doing a job which calls for precision workmanship in a horrifyingly casual manner. It *may* be possible to hire the tools from a Ford dealer, against a deposit to cover their value, especially if you are already a good customer of the garage.

When tackling the overhauls described later in this chapter, the *official* workshop manual (obtainable from your Ford dealer) is also virtually essential. Not only is it necessary to follow the correct procedure during dismantling and reassembly, but the fits and clearances laid down in the manual must be strictly adhered to.

Engine Overhauls. If an engine has covered a very high mileage, a partial overhaul may not restore full power. Instead, it may be necessary to rebore the cylinders and to fit oversize pistons, although rebores are not often necessary nowadays. The crankshaft journals, however, may have to be reground to take undersize connecting-rod and main-bearing shells, and the timing chain and sprockets, and possibly also the oil pump and the starter ring gear, may have to be renewed. Undoubtedly the most satisfactory (and often the cheapest) course in such cases is to fit a works-reconditioned engine, which can be obtained under the service-exchange scheme operated by Ford dealers.

In spite of what has just been said, however, an owner is often persuaded to have a new engine fitted when heavy oil consumption, piston-slap and low oil pressure could have been cured for an expenditure of quite a small sum (seldom exceeding £15–£20), provided that the owner was able to carry out the necessary dismantling and assembly, the worn components being sent to a specialist firm for reconditioning or replacement. If the engine has not covered more than about 40,000 miles, it is worth giving careful consideration to this alternative.

One firm that has made a special study of the effectiveness of reconditioning modern engines in this way is G.M.A. Reconsets Ltd., 119 Uxbridge Road, London, W.12. As a result of their experience, they supply a standard reconditioning kit which includes new pistons, fitted with special oil-control rings (normally rendering reboring unnecessary), a piston-ring compressor, a set of connecting-rod bearing shells, new exhaust valves, a complete set of valve springs, a valve-grinding tool, a timing chain, a complete set of gaskets, gasket cement, an oil filter and graphite assembly compound.

It is not always realized, when trying to assess whether a partial overhaul will be satisfactory, that the condition of the crankshaft is likely to be more important than the amount of wear on the cylinder bores. This is because excessive clearances in the connecting-rod bearings can result in more oil reaching the cylinder walls than can be controlled even by new pistons and special oil-control rings.

If the engine has covered more than 40,000 miles, therefore, it would be as well to enlist the aid of someone who can measure the crankpins with a micrometer. If the wear exceeds 0·001 in., it is advisable to have the crankshaft re-ground. Even half a "thou" of wear can often cause an appreciable increase in oil consumption.

Fitting new connecting-rod bearing shells is usually all that is required, however, when a partial overhaul is undertaken at between 30,000–40,000 miles. In any event, the shells should be replaced as a matter of routine at this mileage.

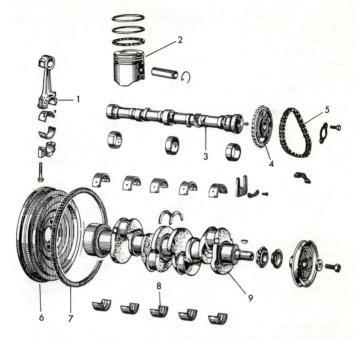

Fig. 50. Engine components of a push-rod engine that may need to be replaced or reconditioned when a partial or major overhaul is carried out. This also applies to the similar components of the overhead-camshaft engine. In addition to these, the valve gear components shown in Figs. 8 and 9 will also require attention

1, connecting rod and bearings; 2, piston, rings and piston-pin assembly; 3, camshaft and bearings; 4, sprocket wheel; 5, timing chain; 6, flywheel; 7, starter ring gear; 8, crankshaft bearings; 9, crankshaft

The bearings are of the thin-shell type which can be installed without the need for skilled fitting. No shims are used and the caps should on no account be filed or rubbed down to take up excessive clearance. Provided that the crankpins are not scored or badly worn, the installation of new bearing shells will give the correct running clearance and restore normal oil pressure.

The main difficulty when dealing with the Cortina engine is that the sump cannot be removed without taking the engine out of the car. When a major overhaul is needed, however, the engine ought to come out anyway.

It must be assumed, of course, that if you are prepared to tackle a partial or a major engine overhaul, you will have had some experience of engine dismantling, fitting and assembly, or will be able to rely on the guidance of an experienced mechanic. The do-it-yourself owner can also learn a lot of the essential "know-how" (which is not necessarily included in a workshop manual, concerned chiefly with dismantling, reassembly and adjustments) from practical handbooks such as *Automobile Workshop Practice*, published in Pitman's Automobile Maintenance Series.

Clutch Overhauls. Fitting a reconditioned clutch assembly should be within the scope of a practical owner but renewal of the clutch pilot bearing in the crankshaft flange calls for the use of special tools and should be left to a Ford dealer. To service the clutch it is necessary to remove the gearbox and clutch housing assembly. The car must, of course, be on axle stands or over a pit.

As it is possible to damage the clutch during removal or assembly, the safest plan is to work strictly to the detailed instructions in the workshop manual, which cannot be reproduced in the space available in this short chapter.

The Steering Gear. What has been said about clutch repairs applies also to overhauls of the steering gear rack-and-pinion unit. An owner can renew the ball joints on the outer ends of the track rods, but dismantling and reassembly of the rack-and-pinion unit is definitely a job for a Ford dealer, as special gauges are needed to adjust the gear and apply the correct pre-load to the pinion and inner ball joints.

The Front Suspension. The front suspension is a fairly simple layout and no great difficulty should be experienced in renewing the various parts, provided that some means of holding the springs compressed can be devised. The safest plan is to use a pair of Ford special tools, to avoid any risk of a makeshift restrainer failing at a critical moment during dismantling or reassembly. If a spring suddenly expands with considerable force, it could cause serious injury to anyone working on the suspension.

The Rear Suspension. The rear suspension, again, should not present many difficulties to an experienced owner but it is advisable to use the special Ford tool to remove and replace the rear suspension bushes.

Index